5
ScottForesman

Accelerating English Language Learning

Authors
Anna Uhl Chamot
Jim Cummins
Carolyn Kessler
J. Michael O'Malley
Lily Wong Fillmore

Consultant
George González

ScottForesman

Editorial Offices: Glenview, Illinois
Regional Offices: Sunnyvale, California • Atlanta, Georgia
Glenview, Illinois • Oakland, New Jersey • Dallas, Texas

Illustrations Unless otherwise acknowledged, all illustrations are the property of Scott, Foresman and Company. Page abbreviations are as follows: (T) top, (B) bottom, (L) left, (R) right, (C) center.

Elizabeth Allen **157**; Susan Burton **114, 225**; Randy Chewning **38, 48**; Sally Comport **214**; George Crespo **168, 171–72** Illustration from HOW THE SEA BEGAN. Three illustrations and cover art copyright © 1993 by George Crespo. Reprinted by permission of Clarion Books/Houghton Mifflin Company. All rights reserved; Michael Dinges **190, 226–227**; Paul Dolan **67**(T), **74**(B), **77, 85, 102–103, 134, 156**; Susan Edison **72, 176, 196–197**; Doris Ettlinger **126–128**; Chuck Gonzales **20–21, 83**; Steve Gillig **10–11, 22-23, 230, 232, 235**; Patti Green **24–25, 45, 71, 152, 166**; Greg Harris **106, 130–131, 135–137**; Rachel Isadora **168, 174** Cover art and illustration from BEN'S TRUMPET by Rachel Isadora. Copyright © 1979 by Rachel Isadora Maioano. By permission of Greenwillow Books, a division of William Morrow and Company, Inc.; Lonnie Sue Johnson **154–155**(C); Laura Kelly **44–45, 63**; Susan Keeter **116–117**; Loretta Krupinski **169** From THE OLD LADIES WHO LIKED CATS by Carol Greene. Illustrated by Loretta Krupinski. Copyright © 1991 by Loretta Krupinski. Cover Copyright © by HarperCollins Publishers. Reprinted by permission of Harper Collins Publishers; Rob Lawson **68–69, 200–201**; Larry McEntire **62**; Yoshi Miyake **16–17**(C), **122–123, 192, 194–195**; Jack Negril **42, 175, 177**(B); Corasue Nicholas **16**(L), **17**(B), **108**(B), **109, 163**; Mark Oldach Design, Ltd **66**(L), **158**; Kathy Petrauskas **40, 177**(T); Mike Reed **100, 216–217, 229**; Joe Rogers **112**; Robert Roth **14**; Susan L. Roth **169** From THE GREAT BALL GAME by Joseph Bruchac, illustrated by Susan L. Roth. Copyright © 1994 by Susan L. Roth. Used by permission of Dial Books for Young Readers, a division of Penguin Books USA Inc.; Barbara Saminich **132, 138–139, 222–223**; John Sandford **12, 112–113, 178–189, 191**(B); Joel Schick **154** Cover art from WAYSIDE SCHOOL IS FALLING DOWN by Louis Sachar. Illustration copyright © 1989 by Joel Schick. Reprinted by permission of Avon Books; Joe Scrofani **2–3**; Andrea Tachiera **104–105, 124–125, 220–221**; Lin Wilson **160–161, 167**(B), **194**(L), **224, 231, 234**.

Literature 26–37: BEN'S TRUMPET by Rachel Isadora. Copyright © 1979 by Rachel Isadora Maiorano. Reprinted by permission of Greenwillow Books, a division of William Morrow and Company, Inc. **50–61:** From HOW WE LEARNED THE EARTH IS ROUND by Patricia G. Lauber. Text copyright © 1990 by Patricia G. Lauber. Illustrations copyright © 1990 by Megan Lloyd. Reprinted by permission of HarperCollins Publishers. **88–99:** HOW THE SEA BEGAN. Text and illustrations copyright © 1993 by George Crespo. Reprinted by permission of Clarion Books/Houghton Mifflin Company. All rights reserved. **140–151:** Reprinted with the permission of Simon & Schuster Books for Young Readers from THE MANY LIVES OF BENJAMIN FRANKLIN. Written down and illustrated by Aliki. Copyright © 1977, 1988 Aliki Brandenberg. **164–165:** From KICKLE SNIFTERS AND OTHER FEARSOME CRITTERS by Alvin Schwartz. Copyright © 1976 by Alvin Schwartz. Illustrations copyright © 1976 by Glen Rounds. Reprinted by permission of HarperCollins Publishers. **178–189:** "A Package for Mrs. Jewls" from WAYSIDE SCHOOL IS FALLING DOWN by Louis Sachar. Copyright © 1989 by Louis Sachar. Reprinted by permission of Lothrop, Lee & Shepard Books, a division of William Morrow and Company, Inc. **202–213:** From SAM THE MINUTEMAN by Nathaniel G. Benchley. Text copyright © 1969 by Nathaniel G. Benchley. Illustrations copyright © 1969 by Arnold Lobel. Reprinted by permission of HarperCollins Publishers.

Poems and Songs 12: "Singing" from EVERYTHING AND ANYTHING by Dorothy Aldis. Copyright © 1925–1927, 1953–1955 by Dorothy Aldis. Reprinted by permission of G.P. Putnam's Sons. **14:** "Come and Sing!" from THE TURQUOISE HORSE, selected by Flora Hood. Copyright © 1972 by Flora Hood. Reprinted by permission of Curtis Brown Ltd. **38:** "Seventy Six Trombones" by Meredith Willson. Copyright © 1957. (Renewed) Frank Music Corp. and Meredith Willson Music. International Copyright Secured. All Rights Reserved. Used by Permission. **62:** "12 October" from THE MALIBU AND OTHER POEMS by Myra Cohn Livingston. Copyright © 1972 Myra Cohn Livingston. Reprinted by permission of Marian Reiner for the author. **76:** "A Horse to Ride" from FEATHERED ONES AND FURRY by Aileen Fisher. Copyright © 1971 by Aileen Fisher. Reprinted by permission of the author. **112:** "Rivers Flow" from THE TURQUOISE HORSE, selected by Flora Hood. Copyright © 1972 by Flora Hood. Reprinted by permission of Curtis Brown Ltd. **166:** "Books to the Ceiling" from WHISKERS & RHYMES by Arnold Lobel. Copyright © 1985 by Arnold Lobel. Reprinted by permission of Greenwillow Books, a division of William Morrow and Company, Inc. **190:** "Good Books, Good Times!" from GOOD BOOKS, GOOD TIMES! by Lee Bennett Hopkins. Copyright © 1985 by Lee Bennett Hopkins. Reprinted by permission of Curtis Brown Ltd.

Photography Unless otherwise acknowledged, all photographs are the property of Scott, Foresman and Company. Page abbreviations are as follows: (T) top, (C) center, (B) bottom, (R) right.

v Superstock; **11** Superstock, Inc.; **13** ©1993 United Feature Syndicate Inc. GARFIELD Comic Strips; **16, 17**(t) David Young-Wolff/PhotoEdit; **17**(b) W.B. Spunbarb/ PhotoEdit; **18** David Young-Wolff/PhotoEdit; **20–21**(b), **24** Superstock, Inc.; **24**(r) Bill Bachman/PhotoEdit; **25** Robert Frerck/Odyssey Productions; **40**(t) Corbis-Bettmann; **40**(b), **41**(tr, c, b) Corbis-Bettmann Archive; **41**(tl) UPI/Corbis-Bettmann; **42** Library of Congress; **42–43** British Museum; **46–47**(c) Corbis-Bettmann Archive; **65, 66–67** Instituto Nacional de Anthropologia e Historia; **70–71** Giraudon/Art Resource; **71** Public Domain; **78–79** ©Tecmap/Westlight; **78**(b) Warren Bolster/Tony Stone Images; **78**(t) Tim Thompson/Tony Stone Images; **79**(b) Darrell Gulin/Tony Stone Images, (cl) Brett Baunton/Tony Stone Images, (t) Willard Clay/Tony Stone Images, (cr) Superstock, Inc.; **80** H. Richard Johnston/Tony Stone Images; **80–81** Superstock, Inc.; **81**(b) George Hunter/Tony Stone Images, (t) Michele & Tom Grimm/Tony Stone Images; **82**(t) Pete Saloutos/Tony Stone Images; **82–83** Art Wolfe/Tony Stone Images; **83**(r) Jeanne Drake/Tony Stone Images; **84**(b) Peter/Stef Laberti/Tony Stone Images, (t) Cathlyn Melloan/Tony Stone Images; **84**(b) Superstock, Inc.; **86** Stephen Frink/Tony Stone Images; **101** H. Richard Johnston/Tony Stone Images; **102–103** Darryl Torckler/Tony Stone Images; **102** Hans Strand/Tony Stone Images; **103** A & L Sinibaldi/Tony Stone Images; **107**(c) Jim Cummins/Tony Stone Images, (b) Tony Stone Images, (t) Ric Ergenbright/Tony Stone Images; **110–111** Tony Stone Images; **111**(b) Nicholas DeVore/Tony Stone Images, (t) ©1983 Robert Caputo/Aurora; **118**(t) Plymouth Plantation Photo, (b) Corbis-Bettmann Archive; **119** Plymouth Plantation Photo; **120**(c) Courtesy of National Life Ins. Co., Montpelier, VT, (t) Museo de America/MAS, (b) Library of Congress; **121**(t) New-York Historical Society; **124** Paulus Leeser, Courtesy Art and Architecture Division, New York Public Library, Astor, Lenox and Tilden Foundations; **125** Superstock, Inc.; **130–131** Superstock, Inc.; **133** Corbis-Bettmann Archive; **154, 155**(b) Superstock, Inc.; **161** ©1991 United Feature Syndicate, Inc.; **192–193** Granger Collection, New York; **192** Corbis-Bettmann Archive; **195, 196** Granger Collection, New York; **197** Corbis-Bettmann Archive; **198**(t) Granger Collection, New York; **198**(b) North Wind Picture Archives; **199** Granger Collection, New York; **216** Brown Brothers; **217**(tr) 'Spirit of '76' by Archibald M. Willard/The original painting hangs in the Selectmen's Room, Abbot Hall, Marblehead, MA/Marblehead Historical Society; **217**(t, tl) Granger Collection, New York; **218**(t, b) Corbis-Bettmann Archive; **219** Granger Collection, New York; **220**(b) North Wind Picture Archives, (t) Corbis-Bettmann Archive; **221**(b), **223**(t) Corbis-Bettmann Archive, (b) Granger Collection, New York; **226** Granger Collection, New York; **227** Paul Conklin/PhotoEdit.

ISBN: 0-673-19672-0

Copyright © 1997

Scott, Foresman and Company, Glenview, Illinois

All Rights Reserved. Printed in the United States of America.

2 3 4 5 6 7 8 9 10 KR 05 04 03 02 01 00 99 98 97

TABLE OF CONTENTS

The Science of Sound

Tell what you know.

Which things in this city are making sound?

What kind of sound does each thing make?

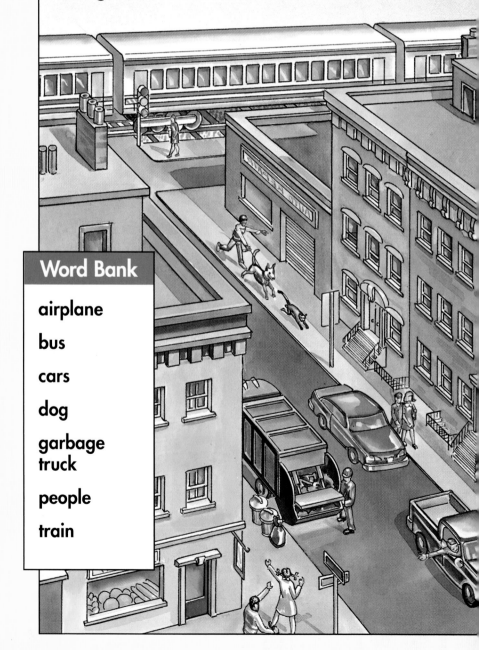

Word Bank

airplane

bus

cars

dog

garbage truck

people

train

Talk About It

What sounds did
you hear on your way
to school today?

3

What is sound?

Sound is anything that you hear.

When an object moves back and forth
quickly, it **vibrates**. The vibrations make
sound waves. When the sound waves
enter your ears, you hear.

Sometimes you can see vibrations.
You can see a rubber band vibrate.
Can you hear it?

Sometimes you can feel vibrations. When you talk or sing, your vocal cords vibrate. Your vocal cords are in your throat. Put your fingers on your throat and sing. Can you feel your vocal cords vibrate?

You can see the way waves travel by touching water with your finger. Circles spread out from where you touch the water. Sound waves travel like this.

Talk About It

Tap your desk with a pencil. Can you hear it? What is vibrating? Make other sounds. What vibrates?

How do you hear?

You hear with your ears.

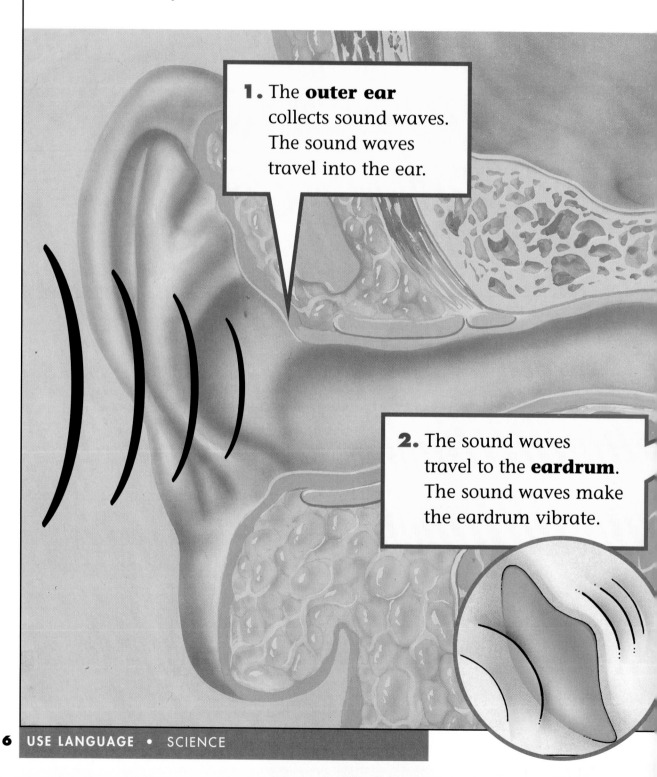

1. The **outer ear** collects sound waves. The sound waves travel into the ear.

2. The sound waves travel to the **eardrum**. The sound waves make the eardrum vibrate.

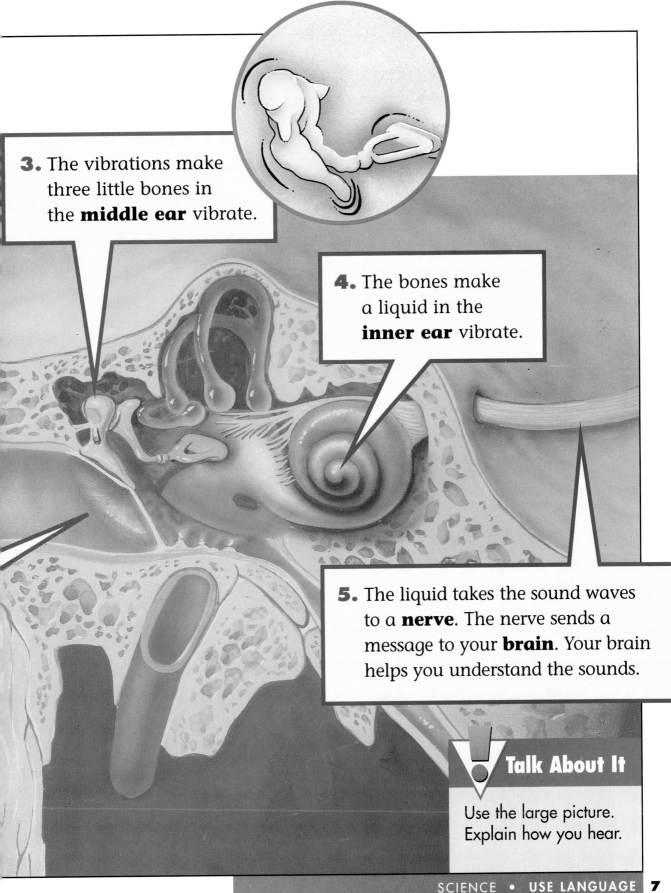

3. The vibrations make three little bones in the **middle ear** vibrate.

4. The bones make a liquid in the **inner ear** vibrate.

5. The liquid takes the sound waves to a **nerve**. The nerve sends a message to your **brain**. Your brain helps you understand the sounds.

Talk About It

Use the large picture. Explain how you hear.

Use an ear trumpet.

Can you make sounds seem louder?
Make an ear trumpet and find out.
An ear trumpet is a cone that people
can use to collect sound waves.

Things You Need

thin sheet of cardboard 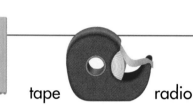 tape  radio

Follow these steps.

1. Roll the cardboard into the shape of a cone. Make the cone wide at one end. Make it narrow at the other end.

2. Tape the sides of the cone to hold it together.

3. Play the radio softly.

4. Point the narrow end of the cone to your ear. Point the wide end of the cone toward the radio. What happens? Does the sound become louder or softer?

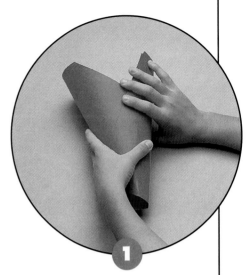

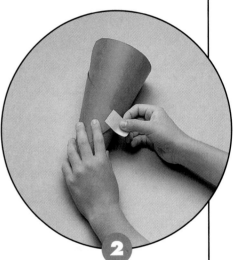

My Record

What happens to sounds when I put the ear trumpet to my ear?

Why does this happen?

Think About It

What do you think would happen if you put the wide part of the ear trumpet to your ear? Why?

How loud is your world?

Volume is how loud or how soft a sound is. Scientists measure volume in **decibels**. A decibel is a unit of measure. Loud sounds have many decibels. Soft sounds have few decibels.

A very loud sound is dangerous. It can hurt your ears. A dangerous sound is measured at more than 130 or 140 decibels.

| 0 | 10 | 20 | 30 | 40 | 50 | 60 | 70 | 80 |

Loudness in Decibels

Use the graph to solve these math problems. Give your answers in decibels.

1. How much louder is the sound of a rock band than the sound of leaves blowing in the wind?

2. How much louder is the sound of a jet engine than the sound of a vacuum cleaner?

Jet engines can make sounds 150 decibels loud. Outside workers at airports wear special earmuffs so the sound does not hurt their hearing.

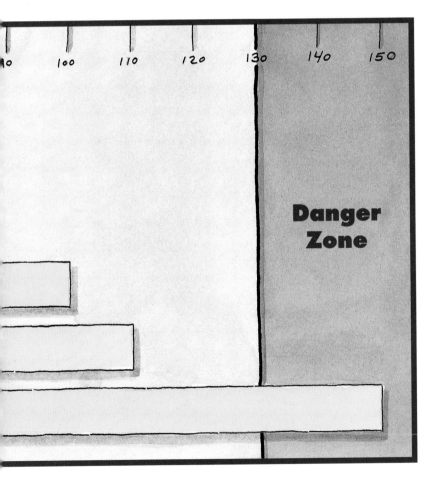

90   100   110   120   130   140   150

Danger Zone

Write About It

Use the graph to write your own math problem. Give your problem to a partner to solve.

Singing

by Dorothy Aldis

Little birds sing with their beaks
In the apple trees;
But crickets in the grass
Are singing with their knees.

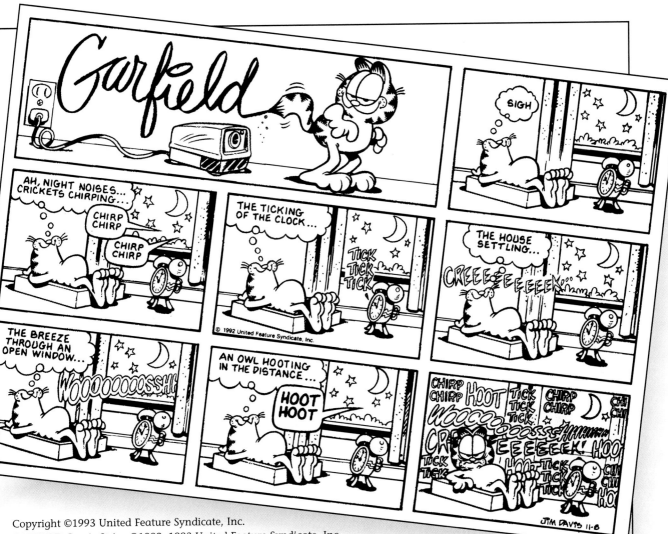

Copyright ©1993 United Feature Syndicate, Inc.
GARFIELD Comic Strips ©1992, 1993 United Feature Syndicate, Inc.

Talk About It

Read the comic strip.

What noises keep Garfield awake at night?

What noises keep you awake at night?

Come and Sing!

a Native American poem

Come and sing!
Come and sing in the old way,
Come and make the juice grow strong
So the corn will grow,
The squash will grow,
The beans will grow.

CONNECT LANGUAGE • SCIENCE/LITERATURE

Tell what you learned.

1. List five objects that make sound.

2. Use the picture on pages 6–7 to explain how you hear sound.

3. Look at the decibels graph on pages 10–11. Name a sound and tell where you would put it on the graph.
For example, a whisper is a soft sound. You can list it near rustling leaves.

4. Garfield heard too many sounds to fall asleep. Draw a picture of something that makes a sound that helps you sleep.

5. What new things did you learn about sound? What else would you like to know about sound?

Uses of Sound

Tell what you know.

What are these people doing?

How is sound helping people?

Word Bank

dancing
directing
explaining
learning
playing
warning

1,467
× 325

7335
2934
4401
476

VENTURA COUNTY
FIRE DEPT.

Talk About It

What sounds do you like to hear?

What sounds let you know about danger?

Vibration and Pitch

Pitch is how high or how low a sound is.

When something vibrates quickly, it makes a high-pitched sound. Most birds make high-pitched sounds.

When something vibrates slowly, it makes a low-pitched sound. A large drum makes a low-pitched sound.

The pitch of some sounds is too high for you to hear. Bats and dolphins hear many sounds that people can't hear.

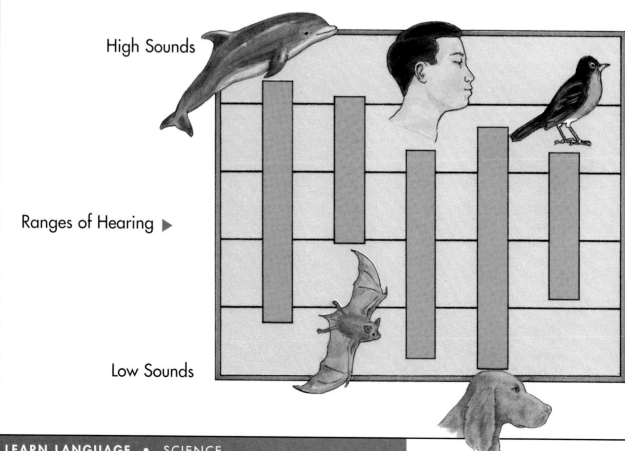

High Sounds

Ranges of Hearing ▶

Low Sounds

You can make sounds of different pitch.

1. Fill one bottle one-quarter full of water.

2. Fill a second bottle half full of water.

3. Fill a third bottle three-quarters full of water.

4. Blow gently across each bottle to vibrate the air inside. Listen to the different sound each bottle makes.

My Record

Which bottle made the highest pitched sound?

Which bottle made the lowest pitched sound?

Why did this happen?

? Think About It

If you filled a bottle to the top and blew gently across it, would you hear a high-pitched sound or a low-pitched sound?

How Musical Instruments Make Sounds

An orchestra usually has three kinds of musical instruments. Each kind of instrument is played in a different way. All the instruments in the orchestra vibrate to make sound.

Stringed instruments can be played by rubbing the strings with a bow. Stringed instruments also can be played by plucking the strings with the fingers. Rubbing or plucking the strings makes the strings vibrate. A violin is a stringed instrument.

Wind instruments are played by blowing into them. Blowing causes the air in the instrument to vibrate. A tuba is a wind instrument.

Percussion instruments are played by hitting or shaking them. The kettledrum is a percussion instrument. The drum vibrates when it is hit.

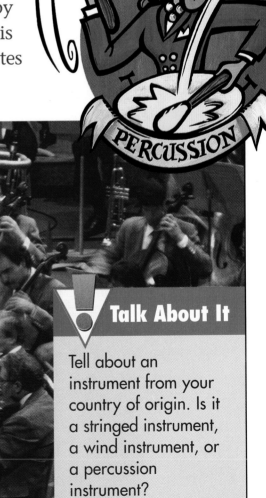

PERCUSSION

Talk About It

Tell about an instrument from your country of origin. Is it a stringed instrument, a wind instrument, or a percussion instrument?

Make a musical instrument.

Instruments make music. Work in a small group to make your own musical instrument. There are three ways you can make sound with your instrument.

- You can pluck the strings of the instrument.

- You can blow into the instrument.

- You can hit or shake the instrument.

Things You Need

plastic cups	pencils	dried beans, marbles
tape	buttons, stones	combs
cans	string	plastic bottles
cookie sheets	wax paper	cardboard tubes
plastic wrap	straws	construction paper
tissue paper	paper plates	seashells
	washers	pieces of cardboard

1. Talk with your group about the sounds the objects can make.

2. Experiment. Put two or three objects together to make sounds.

3. Think about how you can make your instrument better. Can your instrument make sounds with different pitches? Can your instrument make sounds with different volumes?

Write About It

Draw a picture of your instrument. Tell what pieces you used to make it. Describe what sounds it makes.

Making Music Around the World

People everywhere use music to celebrate important events. Songs help all the people at a celebration share the same feelings.

People might celebrate important events with parades. Bands march in parades and play songs. Hearing the music makes listeners want to march too. Did you ever see a parade in your native country? What was the parade for? How did the music make you feel?

People might sing special songs to celebrate birthdays. What song might you hear at a birthday party in your native country?

Special songs are often played at weddings. Songs for dancing might be played at a party for the bride and groom. What songs might be played at a wedding in your native country?

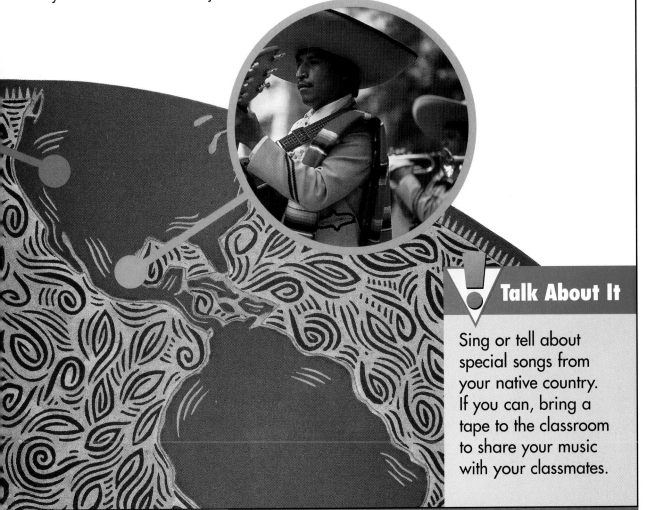

Ben's Trumpet

by Rachel Isadora

In the evening, Ben sits on the fire escape and listens to the music from the Zig Zag Jazz Club. He joins in, playing his trumpet. Sometimes he plays until very late and falls asleep in the hot night air.

Every day on the way home from school,
Ben stops by the Zig Zag Jazz Club.

Language Tip:
Expressions
Stops by means "visits."

He watches the musicians practice.

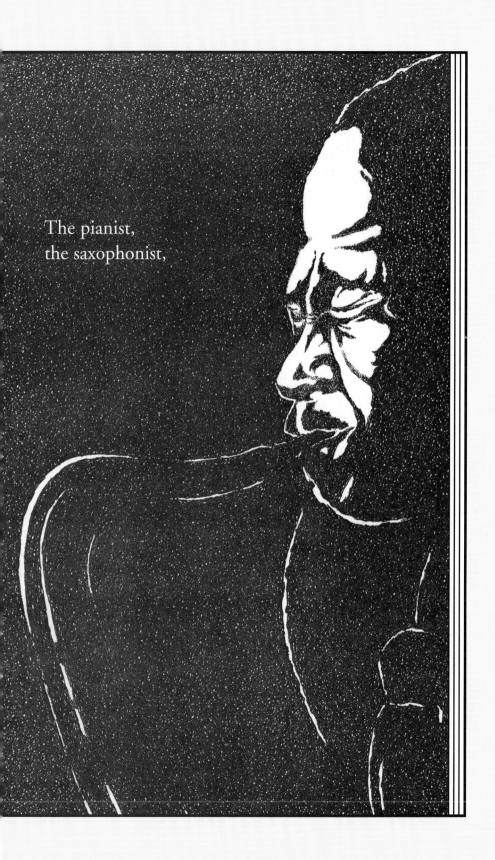

The pianist,
the saxophonist,

the trombonist,

and the drummer.

But most of all Ben thinks the trumpeter is the cat's meow.

Ben feels the rhythm of the music all the way home. He plays for his mama, grandmother and baby brother. And for his papa and his friends.

Language Tip:
Vocabulary
Rhythm is the beat of the music.

Strategy Tip:
Use Pictures for
Meaning
Look at the picture
to understand what
a *stoop* is. What is
Ben sitting on?

Language Tip:
Vocabulary
Horn can mean
"trumpet."

One day, Ben is sitting on the stoop
and playing his trumpet.

"I like your horn," someone says.

It is the trumpeter from the Zig Zag
Jazz Club! Ben smiles and watches him
walk to the Club.

The next day, after school, Ben stops and listens to the musicians practicing a red hot piece. He starts blasting away at his trumpet. Some kids in front of the candy store watch him.

"Hey, what ya doing?" they yell.

Ben stops and turns around.

"What ya think ya doing?" they ask again.

"I'm playing my trumpet," Ben answers.

"Man, you're crazy! You got no trumpet!"

They laugh and laugh.

Ben puts his hands in his pockets and walks slowly home. He sits on the stoop and watches the blinking lights of the Zig Zag Jazz Club. He sits there a long time, just watching.

Down the street the band comes out for a break. The trumpeter comes over to Ben.

"Where's your horn?" he asks.

"I don't have one," Ben says.

The trumpeter puts his hand on Ben's shoulder.

"Come on over to the club," he says, "and we'll see what we can do."

Strategy Tip:
Step into the Story
How do you think
Ben feels now?

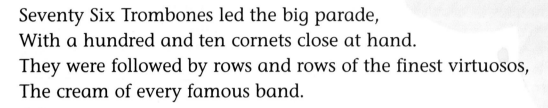

Seventy Six Trombones

from The Music Man
by Meredith Willson

Seventy Six Trombones led the big parade,
With a hundred and ten cornets close at hand.
They were followed by rows and rows of the finest virtuosos,
The cream of every famous band.

Seventy Six Trombones caught the morning sun,
With a hundred and ten cornets right behind.
There were more than a thousand reeds springing up like weeds,
There were horns of every shape and kind.

▼ Try It Out

Ben plays an "air trumpet." Can you play an "air trombone"? Use your imagination. Play an "air" instrument while the other students guess what it is.

Tell what you learned.

1. How are pitch and volume different?

2. Choose your favorite instrument.
Tell a friend how it makes sound.

3. In *Ben's Trumpet,* Ben played a trumpet.
Draw pictures of the other musical
instruments in the jazz group.

4. What have you learned about music
in this chapter? Make an idea web.

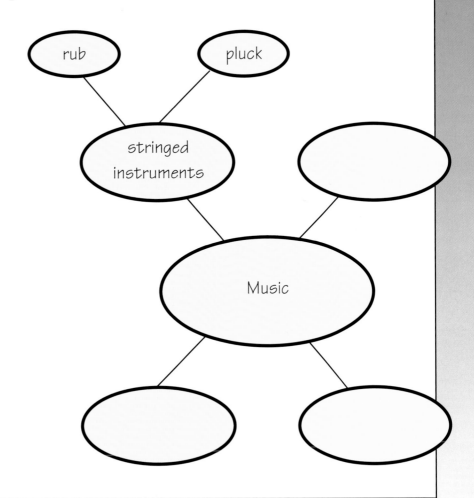

rub

pluck

stringed instruments

Music

The Earth Is Not Flat!

Tell what you know.

Where are these people?

What are they doing?

Word Bank

discovering

exploring

finding

looking for

meeting

searching

traveling

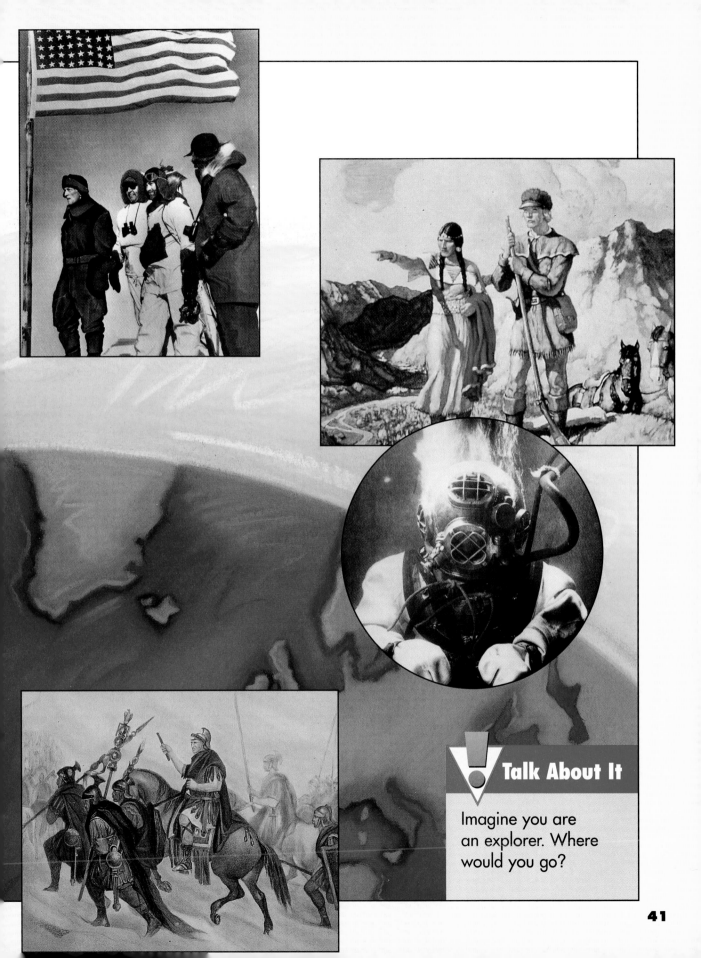

Talk About It

Imagine you are an explorer. Where would you go?

The World of Christopher Columbus

Five hundred years ago, some people believed the earth was flat. They believed a ship that sailed too far could fall off the earth. Other people believed the earth was round.

Christopher Columbus was a map maker and a sailor. He was from Italy. Columbus believed the earth was round.

In the 1400s, India, China, the East Indies, and Japan were called the Indies. The people from Europe bought gold, silk, and spices from the Indies. They sold wool, grain, and salt in the Indies.

| gold | silk | spices | wool | grain | salt |

1492

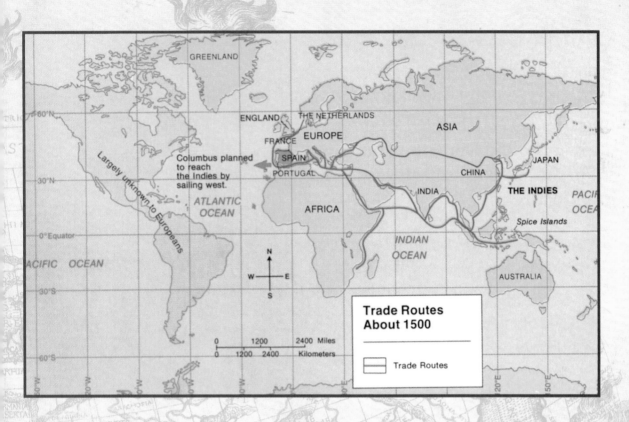

Trade Routes About 1500

The trip to the Indies was hard. Travelers crossed the desert or walked across the mountains. The trip could take a year.

Columbus believed he could find a better way to the Indies. In 1492, the King and Queen of Spain agreed to pay for Columbus's trip.

Try It Out

Look at a globe. Find Spain. Find India, China, and Japan. Find a route you could sail from Spain to India.

Columbus's Voyage

Columbus and his crew left Spain on August 3, 1492. They left in three wooden ships called the Niña, the Pinta, and the Santa María. They sailed west across the Atlantic Ocean.

The crew worked hard on the **voyage**. They raised and lowered the sails. They cleaned the deck. They fixed things. They did not have beds, so they slept on the deck of the ship.

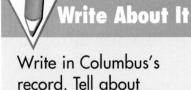

After a month at sea, Columbus's crew felt unhappy and afraid. Each day they traveled further from their homes.

Columbus kept two records of the journey. In one record he wrote about the long distances the ships had traveled. In the other record, he wrote that the ships had traveled shorter distances. This record was for the crew so they would not be afraid. The crew did not know how far they were from home. Then, on October 11, they saw land.

Write About It

Write in Columbus's record. Tell about the day the sailors saw land. How did they feel?

What did Columbus find?

On October 12, Columbus landed on an island in the Caribbean Sea. He named the island San Salvador.

Columbus thought he had landed in the Indies. He called the people living on the island Indians. These American Indians were probably Taino people. The Taino people were farmers who grew corn and yams.

The Indians greeted Columbus and his men with water, food, parrots, and balls of cotton. The sailors gave the Indians glass beads and small bells.

The Indians taught the sailors about **hammocks**. Hammocks are woven beds that hang from ropes. Hammocks could be used for sleeping on the ship.

But not everything was good. Many Indians caught diseases from the sailors. Columbus also took Indians back to Spain to work as slaves.

Word Bank

faces

hands

signs

acting

pointing

talking

Talk About It

The sailors and the Indians spoke different languages. How do you think they communicated?

How did Columbus find his way?

Christopher Columbus used a **compass** to find his way. A compass helps people know the direction they are going.

A compass's needle is a **magnet**. A magnet is made of iron or steel. It attracts, or pulls to it, other small pieces of iron or steel. A magnet can also attract other magnets.

The earth is like a big magnet. It has magnetic poles called the North Magnetic Pole and the South Magnetic Pole. The needle of a compass always points toward the earth's magnetic poles.

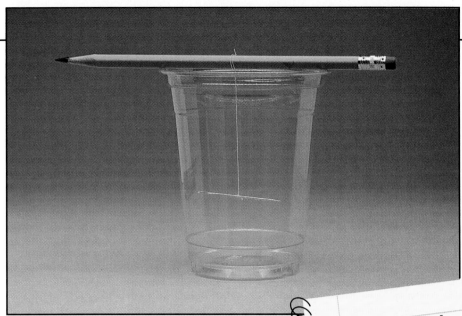

You can make a compass.

1. Rub a magnet twenty times across a needle. Always rub in the same direction.

2. Cut a short thread. Tie one end around the center of the needle. Tie the other end around the center of a pencil.

3. Place the pencil across a glass. The needle will soon point north-south.

My Record

Here is a chart of things that are in the north, south, east, and west parts of my classroom.

North
South
East
West

Think About It

How can you check whether your needle has become a magnet?

How We Learned the Earth Is Round

by
Patricia Lauber

illustrated by
Megan Lloyd

Strategy Tip:
Stop and Think
Look out the window.
Does the earth look
round or flat?

Today nearly everybody knows
that the earth is round.

But long ago, people were sure
the earth was flat. They thought it was
flat because it looked flat. It still does.

Strategy Tip:
Use Pictures for
Meaning
The picture can help
you understand that
a prairie is a large area
of land with grass, but
no trees.

Stand out on the prairie. Sail out onto the ocean. You can see for miles, and the earth looks flat.

Climb a mountain. Now the earth looks rough and bumpy, but it doesn't seem to curve. It doesn't look round.

The earth looks flat because it is big and we are small. We see only a tiny piece at one time. The tiny piece does curve, but the curve is too slight for our eyes to see. And that is why, for thousands of years, people thought the earth was flat.

Language Tip:
Opposites
The words *flat* and *curved* are opposites. If something is *flat*, it is not curved. If something is *curved*, it is not flat.

The earth's real shape was discovered about 2,500 years ago. The people who discovered it were Greeks.

At first the Greeks, too, believed the earth was flat. But certain Greeks were great thinkers. They thought hard about things they saw and tried to explain them. They asked themselves questions—Why? What if? And then they thought some more.

Everybody knew that a strange thing happened when a ship left harbor. As it sailed away, it appeared to sink. First the hull disappeared, then the bottom of the sail, then the top.

As a ship returned, it seemed to rise out of the sea. First the sail appeared, then the hull.

The Greeks wondered why.

Strategy Tip:
Use Context
If you don't know the word *hull*, try reading the whole sentence. The picture might help too.

Why didn't the whole ship just get smaller and smaller or bigger and bigger? That's what should happen on a flat earth.

But it didn't happen. Why didn't it?

Perhaps the answer had to do with the shape of the earth. Perhaps the earth wasn't flat after all. Perhaps it had some other shape.

What if the earth had a curved surface? What would happen to a ship then?

You can see what happens yourself. Use a big ball and a ship made from an eraser, a toothpick, and a piece of paper. With one hand, hold the ball in front of you at eye level. Use the other hand to move the ship.

When a ship sails away over a curved surface, the bottom disappears first. When it returns, the top appears first.

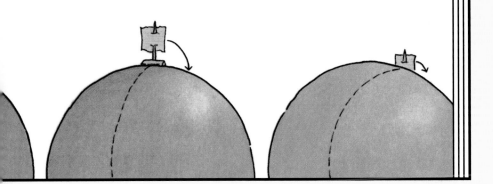

The Greeks decided the earth must have a curved surface. That would explain why ships seemed to sink and rise.

They also saw that the same thing happened no matter which way a ship was heading—east, west, north, or south. The earth must curve in all directions.

Was it round? They found the answer in the night sky.

Strategy Tip:
Make Predictions
How can the night sky show that the earth curves in all directions?

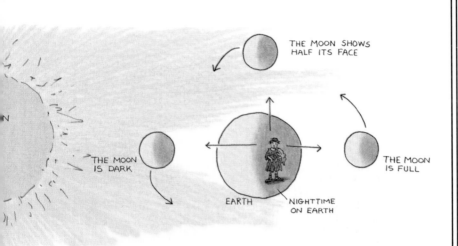

THE MOON SHOWS
HALF ITS FACE

THE MOON
IS DARK

THE MOON
IS FULL

EARTH

NIGHTTIME
ON EARTH

The Greeks had studied the skies for many years. They knew that the sun made its own light and the moon did not. The moon shone because it reflected light from the sun.

They also knew that the moon traveled around the earth. As it did so, different parts of it were lighted up by the sun. That was why the moon seemed to change its shape, why they might see a sliver of moon, a bigger piece, or a full moon. They saw a full moon whenever the moon was on the far side of the earth from the sun.

Language Tip:
Irregular Verbs
Shone is the past tense of shine.

Strategy Tip:
Cause and Effect
To reflect means "to throw back." The moon has no light of its own. It shines because it reflects the sun's light.

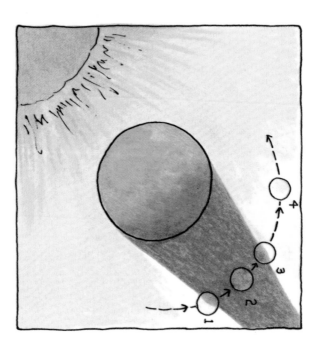

But sometimes a shadow dimmed the light of a full moon—an eclipse took place. The shadow seemed to sweep across the face of the moon. The edge of the shadow was curved. It was like part of a circle.

The Greeks knew that this shadow was the earth's. It was the shadow that the earth cast in space. When the moon moved through the shadow, an eclipse took place.

Language Tip:
Special Vocabulary
To cast a shadow means "to make a shadow." A shadow is made when an object blocks a bright light.

Sometimes the moon was high in the sky during an eclipse. Sometimes it was low. Yet as long as the sun, earth, and moon were lined up, an eclipse took place. And the edge of the shadow was always the same curve.

There is only one shape that always casts the same shadow. That shape is round. A ball, for example, always casts the same shadow no matter how it is turned. It casts the same shadow no matter where the light is coming from.

And that is how the Greeks found out the earth is round.

Strategy Tip:
Summarizing
Can you explain why an eclipse helped the Greeks understand that the earth was round?

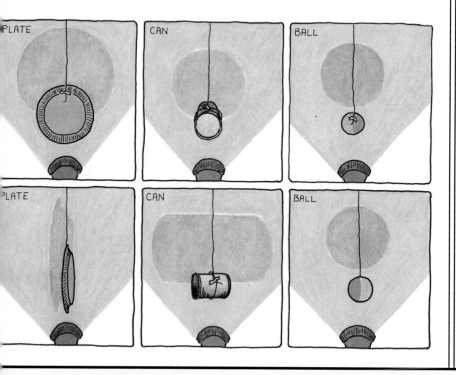

12 October

by Myra Cohn Livingston

From where I stand now
   the world is flat,
   flat out flat,
   no end to that.

   Where my eyes go the land moves out.

How is it then
five hundred years ago (about)
Columbus found
that far beyond the flat on flat
the world was round?

Tell what you learned.

1. If you were a map maker, how would you change the map of the world in 1493?

2. Work with a partner to draw pictures showing Columbus and his trip to America.

3. Explain to a partner how you know the earth is round. Draw pictures and use objects to help you.

4. What did you learn about Columbus? What would you like to know more about?

CHAPTER 4

The Aztecs and the Spaniards

Tell what you know.

How are these two cities the same?

How are they different?

Word Bank

buildings

mules

roads

roofs

stairs

towers

Talk About It

In what ways are these cities like the place you live?

The Aztec City of Tenochtitlán

In 1325, the Aztecs built the city of Tenochtitlán. They built it on an island in the middle of a lake. They built it in the area that is Mexico City today.

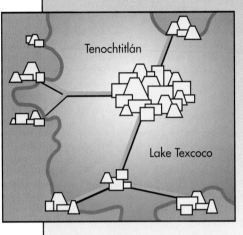

According to a story, a god told the Aztec people where to build their city. The god told the Aztec people to look for a special island. On the island they would find a cactus growing from a rock. They would find an eagle standing on the cactus. The eagle would have a snake in its mouth.

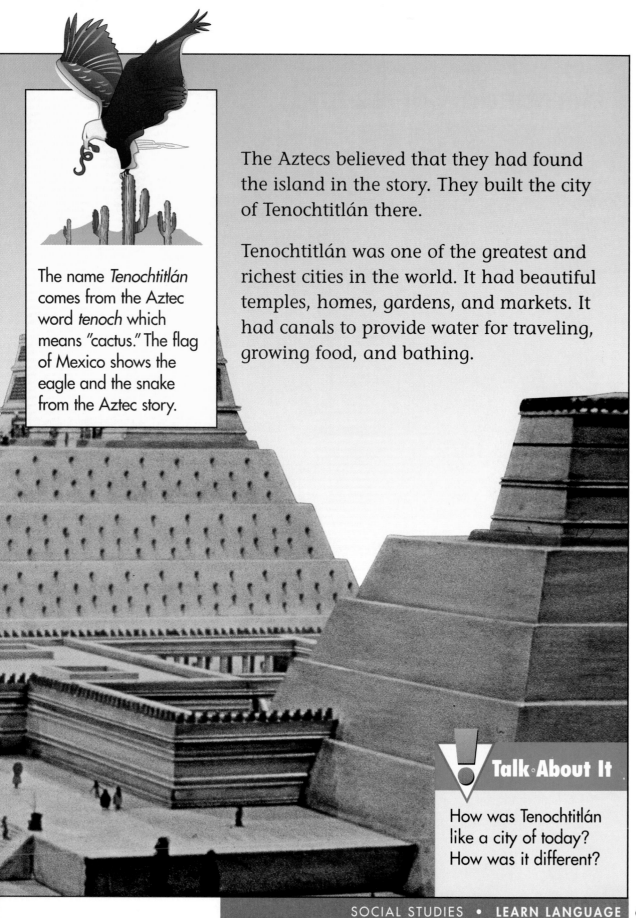

The name *Tenochtitlán* comes from the Aztec word *tenoch* which means "cactus." The flag of Mexico shows the eagle and the snake from the Aztec story.

The Aztecs believed that they had found the island in the story. They built the city of Tenochtitlán there.

Tenochtitlán was one of the greatest and richest cities in the world. It had beautiful temples, homes, gardens, and markets. It had canals to provide water for traveling, growing food, and bathing.

Talk About It

How was Tenochtitlán like a city of today? How was it different?

Hernando Cortés finds Tenochtitlán.

Hernando Cortés was a Spanish explorer. He heard stories about a city of gold in Mexico. In 1519, Cortés decided to find it.

Cortés had an army of six hundred men. His men had guns, dogs, and large horses. The Aztecs who saw Cortés knew they could not fight him and win.

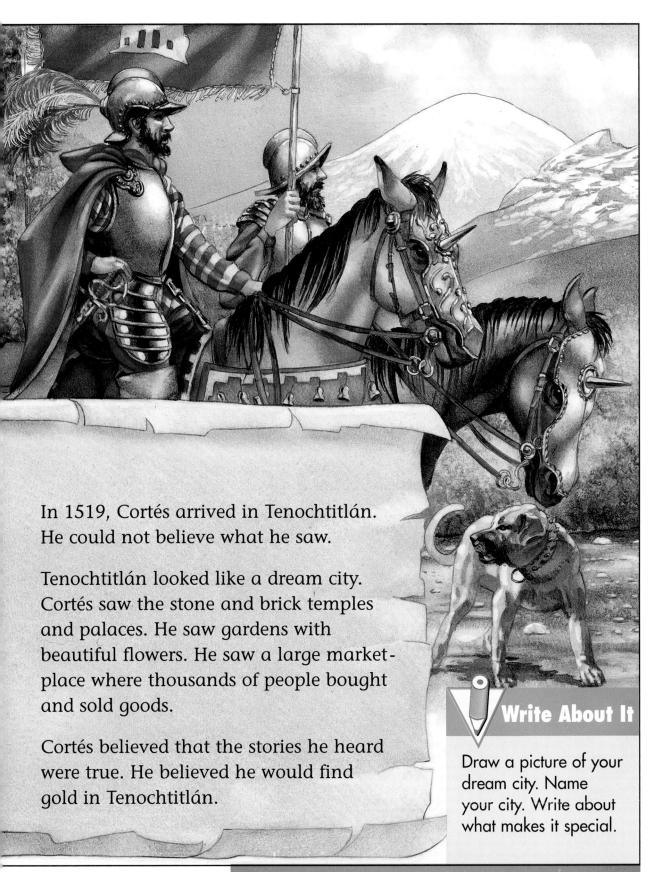

In 1519, Cortés arrived in Tenochtitlán. He could not believe what he saw.

Tenochtitlán looked like a dream city. Cortés saw the stone and brick temples and palaces. He saw gardens with beautiful flowers. He saw a large market-place where thousands of people bought and sold goods.

Cortés believed that the stories he heard were true. He believed he would find gold in Tenochtitlán.

Write About It

Draw a picture of your dream city. Name your city. Write about what makes it special.

Cortés and the Aztecs

Montezuma, the Aztec emperor, heard stories too. He heard that one day the great Aztec god, Quetzalcoatl, would return from the sea. He heard that Quetzalcoatl would look like a man and have light skin and a beard. Montezuma thought that Cortés might be Quetzalcoatl.

Montezuma gave Cortés many gifts. But Cortés wanted to rule the Aztecs. He wanted their gold and jewels. Soon Cortés began to fight the Aztecs.

There were many fights between Cortés's army and the Aztecs. Many people were killed. Finally, Cortés's army won. They destroyed the city of Tenochtitlán. Cortés conquered the Aztecs.

Think About It

Imagine that you are an Aztec. How is your life different after Cortés has won?

The Horse

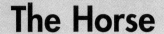

Cortés brought horses to America.
Horses are beautiful and useful animals.

A horse grows a thick **coat** of hair
in the fall and sheds it in the spring.

A horse has long, strong legs that
help it pull heavy loads and run fast.

A horse's feet also help it run.
Its foot is really a large toe. The tip
of the toe is covered by the **hoof**.
The tip of the toe is the only part
of the foot that touches the ground.

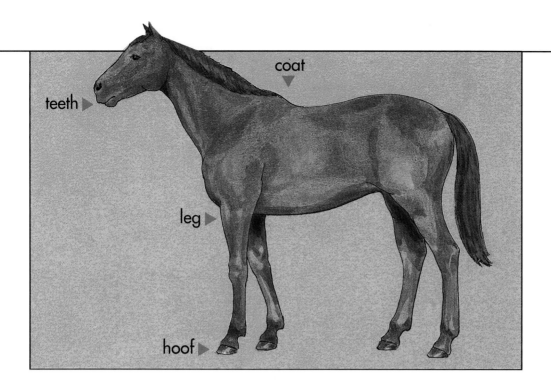

teeth ▶

coat ▼

leg ▶

hoof ▶

Horses have strong teeth. They eat grain and plants. An expert can find out a horse's age by counting its teeth and seeing if they are worn down.

Horses can learn commands. A horse can learn to come when it hears a whistle. A horse can learn to move forward when the rider presses his or her legs against the horse's sides.

Word Bank

circuses

horse shows

parades

rodeos

farming

ranching

horseback riding

 Talk About It

In the past, horses provided the fastest way to travel on land. How do people use horses today?

Make an Aztec sun god mask.

To honor the sun god, the Aztecs made **mosaic** masks from turquoise stones, jade, and shells. A mosaic is a picture or design made by fitting together small pieces.

You can make a sun god mask. Get these things ready.

Things You Need

salt dough   eggshells   paintbrush   glue

blue or black tempera paint   food coloring   paper towels

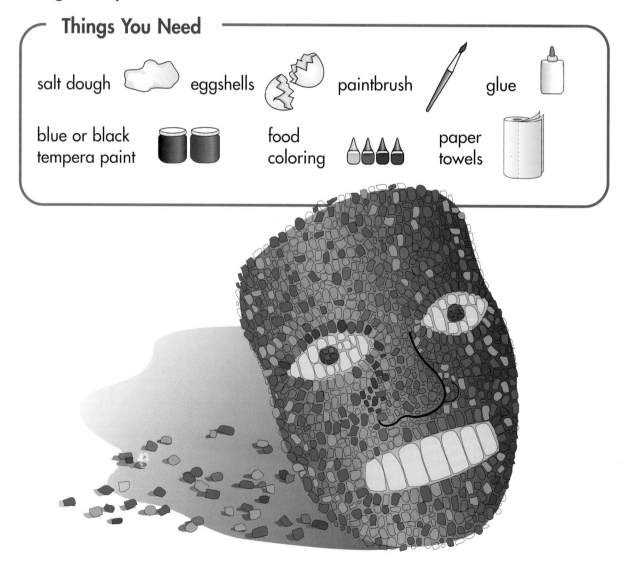

Follow these steps.

1. Break the eggshells into small pieces. Use food coloring to make the pieces different colors.

2. Dry the colored eggshell pieces on paper towels.

3. Prepare salt dough.

4. Shape the dough into a mask. Let your mask dry in the sun.

5. Paint your mask with black or blue paint. Let the paint dry.

6. Glue on colored eggshell pieces to decorate your mask. Look at the picture for ideas.

Salt Dough Recipe

1 cup salt
2 cups flour
1 cup water
2-3 drops vegetable oil

Mix these things together and roll out the dough.

Try It Out

Find a partner.
Use your Aztec masks
to tell a story.

A Horse to Ride

by Aileen Fisher

Sometimes a horse
has a rumpled hide,
or a sway in his back,
or his back's too wide
for my sort of legs
to sit astride,

But I wouldn't care
how he looked *outside*
if I only, only, only
had a horse to ride.

Tell what you learned.

1. Describe the city of Tenochtitlán.
Draw a picture to help you tell about it.

2. Would you like to have a horse?
Tell why or why not.

3. You followed the directions to make
an Aztec mask. Give a partner directions
on how to make or do something.

4. What did you learn about Cortés
and the Aztecs? What else would you
like to know?

Precious Water

Tell what you know.

You can see water in many places.

What do you see in the pictures?

Word Bank

lake

ocean

pond

puddle

river

stream

waterfall

Was there a body of water near your family's home in your country of origin?

Is there a body of water near where you live now?

Salt Water and Fresh Water

Most of the earth is covered with water. Most of the earth's water is in the oceans. There are four oceans on earth. They are the Pacific, Atlantic, Indian, and Arctic Oceans. Look at a globe to see how they are connected.

Ocean water is salty. You cannot use salt water for drinking, cooking, or washing. There is so much salt in ocean water that drinking it can make you sick. Washing metal things in the ocean's water causes them to rust.

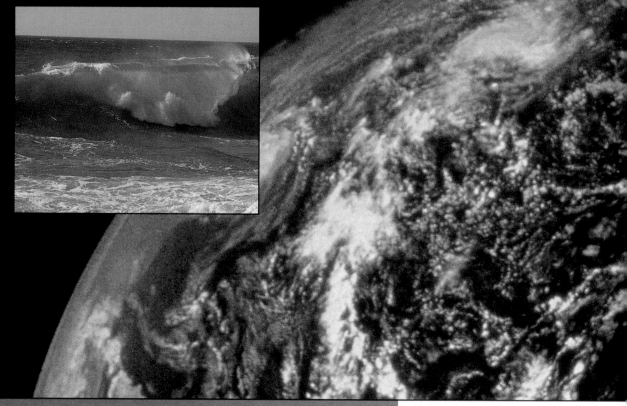

Only a small amount of the earth's water is fresh. Most fresh water is in the form of ice at the North and South Poles. The rest of the earth's fresh water is in rivers and lakes. It is also underground. You can use fresh water for drinking, cooking, and washing.

Write About It

What do you think of when you think of the ocean? Draw a picture and write about it.

All living things need water.

People, animals, and plants need water to stay alive. They need water to live and grow.

Farmers need water to grow **crops**. They also need water for the animals that they raise. In dry places, farmers must **irrigate**. They must water their fields.

People need water to stay clean. People use water to wash themselves. They use water to wash their clothes and dishes.

Some animals use water to wash their food. Some animals use water to stay cool.

? Think About It

Talk with a friend. Why is water important to you? Do you and your friend agree?

How do people use water?

People use water to get from one place to another. They use oceans, lakes, and rivers as roads. People travel by water for work and for vacations. Some people travel by water to find a new home.

People use water to move things from one place to another. Ships can carry things shorter distances, such as across a lake, or longer distances, such as across an ocean.

People use animals from the oceans, lakes, and rivers as sources of food. They eat fish, shrimp, and lobsters.

People use water for having fun. They play games and relax in the water. They play sports in the water. They cool off in the water in hot weather.

What are the people in the picture above doing?

Word Bank

canoeing

fishing

sailing

swimming

water-skiing

 Try It Out

What is the class's favorite way to have fun in the water? Do a class survey. Record the responses on a graph.

Salty Water

You know that there is salt in the oceans because you can smell it. You can taste it too. Have you ever swallowed a mouthful of ocean water when you were swimming in the ocean? How did it taste?

Try this experiment. It will show you
if salt is in water.

Things You Need

2 shallow pans    1 teaspoon of salt   1 cup of warm water

Follow these steps.

1. Fill each pan with 1/2 cup
of the warm water.

2. Put the salt in one of the pans.
Stir the water until the salt dissolves.
What happens to the salt?

3. Leave both pans until all the
water dries up.

4. What is left in each pan after
the water dries up?

My Record

What happened to the salt
after I stirred the water?

What was left in each pan
after the water dried up?

Why did this happen?

 Think About It

How could people
make ocean water
good to drink?

How The Sea Began

a Taino myth retold and illustrated by George Crespo

Reader's Tip
A myth is a story that explains something. People pass along myths from one generation to another.

In the beginning of time, before the land was surrounded by sea, in a place called Zuania, there were four great mountains. One mountain was called Boriquén, Land of Brave Men. And on that mountain, in the village of Coabey, lived an old man named Yaya with his wife, Itiba, and their only son, Yayael. Yayael was a skilled hunter.

Yayael hunted with a bow that his father had carved for him out of tabonuco wood. It is said that the tabonuco tree is the home of spirits, and that its wood holds magical powers.

This saying may be true, because when Yayael went out hunting he always brought back game. The people of Coabey ate well, even when the other hunters came back empty-handed.

Strategy Tip:
Look for a Familiar
Word
*Lowering clouds are
clouds that become
low in the sky. Lowering
clouds make the
sky darker.*

Strategy Tip:
Read On
*To understand what
a hurricane is, read
through the first
paragraph on page 91.*

One day while Yayael was out hunting he saw that the sky was darkening in the east. A flock of swallows flying before the lowering clouds circled around his head, flapping and beating their wings. Yayael knew this was a warning that Guabancex, the terrible goddess of hurricanes, was coming. He quickly hid his bow and arrows under a large rock and ran toward the village, hoping to reach safety before the winds overtook him.

Guabancex created a hurricane that struck with tremendous force. The winds howled and raged for hours. The villagers who had been working in their fields sought shelter in a cave nearby. Yaya and Itiba prayed to the supreme god Yúcahu that Yayael would come through the storm unharmed.

When the winds died down, the people thanked Yúcahu, then ventured from the cave. They found that their huts had been flattened by the storm. Yaya and Itiba waited, but Yayael did not appear.

Language Tip:
Vocabulary
Sought is the past tense of seek. Seek means "to look for."

Strategy Tip:
Look for a Familiar Word
Flattened huts are huts that have been made flat.

Yaya went to search for his son. He found the bow and arrows where Yayael had hidden them, but of Yayael himself there was no sign.

When Itiba saw her husband returning with their son's bow and arrows in his hands, she called out Yayael's name. Then she fell down weeping at her husband's feet.

Yaya reverently placed Yayael's bow and arrows in a large gourd. Then he sat down beside his wife and wept too.

Strategy Tip:
Use Pictures for Meaning
A *gourd* is a large fruit. This gourd has been cut in half and dried out. It is being used as a bowl.

Strategy Tip:
Make Inferences
How can you tell that Yayael's parents believe he is dead?

The villagers helped one another rebuild their homes. When the time for grieving was over, they helped Yaya and Itiba hang the gourd from the ceiling of their hut, where the bow and arrows would be safe, just in case Yayael's spirit should wish to visit them. Yaya picked up his own bow and arrows and went to hunt, for now the village could no longer depend on Yayael to bring home meat.

Strategy Tip:
Use Picture Clues
To understand grieving, look at the illustration on page 92. How do Yayael's parents feel?

Strategy Tip:
Summarizing
What has happened to Yayael and his family?

Strategy Tip:
Use Context Clues
Seldom means "not often." You can figure this out by reading the sentence that follows: "All were hungry."

Though the men of the village hunted every day, they seldom brought home enough for everyone. All were hungry. Even the children, who were always fed first, were becoming thin and sickly.

One evening Yaya asked Itiba to lower the gourd that held Yayael's weapons. "I want to see our son's bow," he said. "Perhaps it still holds the power of the tabonuco."

As Itiba lowered the gourd to the floor, it tipped just a little. Out spilled many beautiful, plump fish. Yaya and Itiba were astonished. They had never before seen such fish—large and silvery and still breathing, as if freshly taken from the water. Itiba cooked them and invited the whole village to share the meal.

The villagers rejoiced in their good fortune. They sang, "Baharí Yayael"—We honor you, Yayael—and went to bed with full stomachs.

Language Tip:
Vocabulary
To stand on tiptoe
means "to stand
with only your toes
on the ground."

The following day, all the villagers went out to work in the fields. They left four boys to guard the gourd that held Yayael's bow and arrows, the bow and arrows that turned into fish.

The boys were curious and hungry. The higher the sun climbed into the sky, the more curious and hungry they became. One boy stood up on tiptoe and tried to peer into the gourd. Then a second boy tried to climb up and see inside. They were joined by the other two, and together they brought the gourd down to the floor. Out flopped four fish, just the right size for four hungry boys.

The boys cooked the fish and ate them. Then they ate four more. They sang praises to Yayael's spirit and lowered the gourd again for more fish.

Suddenly the boys heard Yaya and the villagers returning from the fields. Afraid of being caught, they hurried to raise the gourd to the ceiling.

In their haste, they failed to secure the rope that held the gourd in its place. The gourd fell to the ground and broke open.

Language Tip:
Vocabulary
To secure means "to fasten or tie something well."

Strategy Tip:
Summarize
What has happened to Yayael's bow and arrows?

Strategy Tip:
Make Inferences
Why did the water
taste salty like tears?
Whose tears were they?

Water rushed out of the broken gourd. In an instant everything in the hut was afloat. A wave swept the boys out of the hut and out of the village and left them, choking and sputtering, on the path that led to the fields. There Yaya and the other villagers found them; the water tasted of salt, the boys said, like the salt of tears.

Water continued to flow from the gourd. It flowed and rose to cover the land. And fish swam out of the gourd—large fish and small fish, starfish, urchins, and jellyfish, all kinds of sea creatures came out of the gourd to fill the water with life.

The villagers gathered on the mountaintop
and watched as the waters covered Zuania.
When at last the water stopped rising, they saw
that their mountain, Boriquén, was now an island.
They gave their thanks to Yúcahu, dressed themselves
festively, and celebrated with music and dancing,
because as long as there were fish in the sea,
they would not go hungry.

And this is one story of how the sea began.

Strategy Tip:
Stop and Think
How did Yayael,
the hunter, help his
people again?

Sailing Song

a sea chantey

Hey, ho, I like the ocean,
Hey, ho, I like the ocean,
Hey, ho, I like the ocean,
Early in the morning.

I'll ride the rolling waves,
I'll ride the rolling waves,
I'll ride the rolling waves,
Early in the morning.

Pull rope, and up the anchor,
Pull rope, and up the anchor,
Pull rope, and up the anchor,
Early in the morning.

Tell what you learned.

1. List three ways that people use water.

2. Why do people use fresh water
for drinking, cooking, and washing?

3. Draw pictures of what happens
in *How the Sea Began*. Write about
each picture. Use your pictures
to retell the story to a friend.

4. What did you learn about water?

The Forms of Water

Tell what you know.

Can you find the water in each picture?

▲ glacier

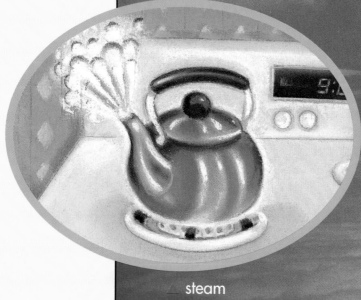

steam

clouds

snow

waterfall

Talk About It

How do you use
different forms
of water?

103

Water can be a solid, a liquid, or a gas.

Water has different forms at different temperatures. Water can be a **solid**, a **liquid**, or a **gas**.

When the temperature is below freezing (0° C or 32° F), water is a solid. Ice is the solid form of water.

When the temperature is above freezing, water is a liquid. Lakes, rivers, streams, and oceans are filled with water. Some of this water comes from snow and ice that melts on mountains. Some comes from rain.

When the temperature of water rises, the water **evaporates**, or disappears into the air. The liquid water changes into a gas. **Water vapor** is the gas form of water.

There is water vapor in the air you breathe. Blow on a mirror to see the water vapor in your breath.

Write About It

Have you seen water change forms? Write about what you saw. Tell why the water changed forms.

The Water Cycle

The earth has the same amount of water now as it had in the days of the dinosaurs. The water on earth is used again and again. It goes through a cycle of changes called the **water cycle**.

Water moves from the earth to the sky and back to the earth. As it moves, it changes form. The heat of the sun makes water change its form.

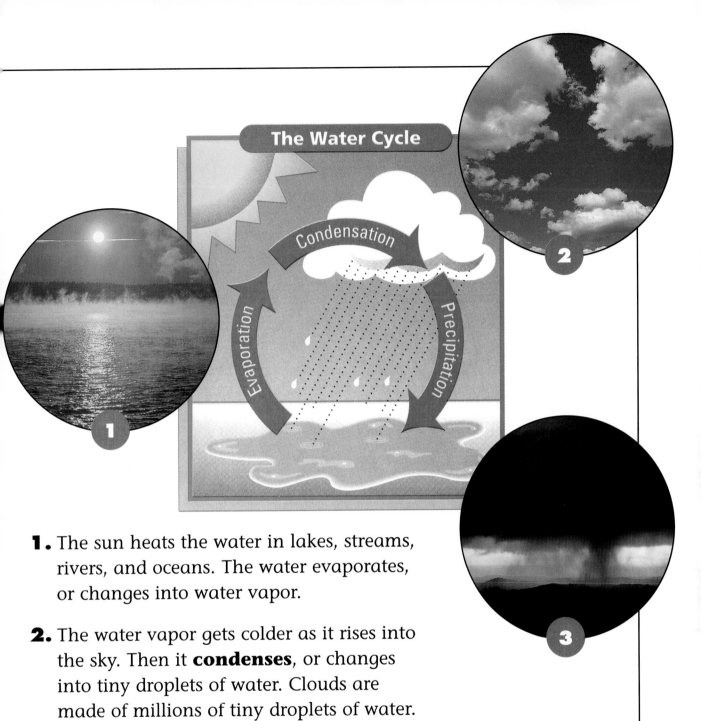

The Water Cycle

Condensation

Evaporation

Precipitation

1. The sun heats the water in lakes, streams, rivers, and oceans. The water evaporates, or changes into water vapor.

2. The water vapor gets colder as it rises into the sky. Then it **condenses**, or changes into tiny droplets of water. Clouds are made of millions of tiny droplets of water.

3. When the droplets of water become heavy, they fall from the clouds as rain or snow. This is called **precipitation**. The water goes back into the rivers, lakes, and oceans.

Talk About It

Work with a partner to describe the water cycle.

A Water Cycle Experiment

Things You Need

ice cube

clock

sunny area

small dish

marker

Follow these steps.

1. Place the ice cube on the dish.

2. Place the dish in a sunny area.

3. Record the time and date.

4. Watch the ice cube melt.

2:00 P.M.
Put ice cube
in sun.

5. Write the time when the ice is completely melted. Mark the dish at the edge of the water.

6. Watch the water to see if it evaporates.

7. Write the time when you first notice the water is completely evaporated.

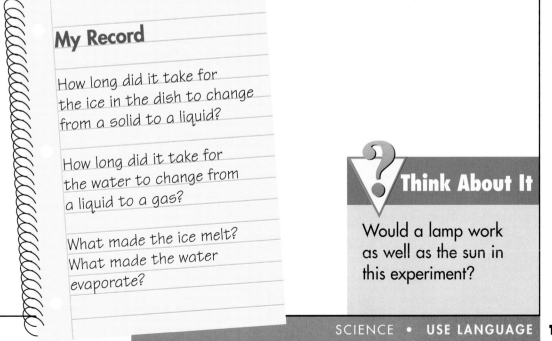

My Record

How long did it take for the ice in the dish to change from a solid to a liquid?

How long did it take for the water to change from a liquid to a gas?

What made the ice melt? What made the water evaporate?

Think About It

Would a lamp work as well as the sun in this experiment?

Water and the Sahara Desert

The largest desert in the world is the Sahara Desert in Africa. It is about the same size as the United States. The desert spreads into eleven countries.

Look at the picture of the desert. How would you describe it?

Word Bank

camels

palm trees

sand

shrubs

villages

dry

hot

The Sahara Desert is dry. Little rain falls in the desert. Few plants grow there.

Egypt is in the Sahara Desert. Almost all the people in Egypt live near the Nile River. Farmers dig shallow ditches to bring river water to their crops.

An Egyptian village on the Nile River.

An **oasis** is a place in the desert where people find water. Ponds and underground springs wet the desert soil. Plants grow there. Palm trees grow there. Farmers can grow crops at a large oasis.

An oasis in the Sahara Desert.

Write About It

Draw a picture of an oasis. Then write about your picture.

Rivers Flow

a Native American poem

Rivers flow.
The sea sings.
Oceans roar.
Tides rise.
Who am I?
A small pebble
On a giant shore;
Who am I
To ask who I am?
Isn't it enough to be?

Who Am I?

Anonymous

Who am I?
I come from the sky;
I wash the grass,
And over the road
You may hear me pass.
The flowers all love me
So do the trees—
I make the brooks sing
As they run to the seas.

Rain

by Robert Louis Stevenson

The rain is raining all around,
It falls on field and tree,
It rains on the umbrellas here,
And on the ships at sea.

Tell what you learned.

1. Draw a diagram of the water cycle. Use it to explain how the water cycle works. Include the following words in your explanation: evaporate, condense, precipitation.

2. Where do people find water in the Sahara Desert?

3. What words would you use in a poem about water? Make an idea web like the one below.

4. What did you like best about this chapter?

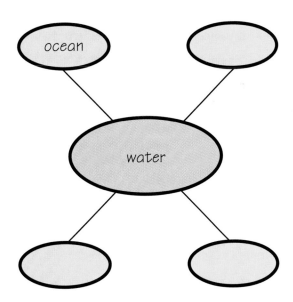

CHAPTER 7

Coming to America

Tell what you know.

These people came to America in the 1600s.

How did they get here?

Why do people come to America?

Word Bank

farms
freedom
jobs
land
money
religion

Talk About It

How did your family
come to America?

The Early Settlers

a reproduction of the Mayflower II, a ship used by early settlers

Christopher Columbus landed in America in 1492. He found a part of the world that most Europeans didn't know about.

After Columbus's voyage, explorers from several countries in Europe came to America. They told people at home about the new land. Soon, other people were interested in coming to America too.

In the late 1500s and early 1600s, small groups of Europeans began to come to America to live. They lived in different parts of the country. They were called **settlers**.

Many of the early settlers were from Spain, England, France, the Netherlands, and Sweden. When each group of settlers arrived in America, they lived together in the same area. They lived in **colonies**. A colony is an area of land that is settled by people who come from the same country.

▲ a reconstructed early settlement

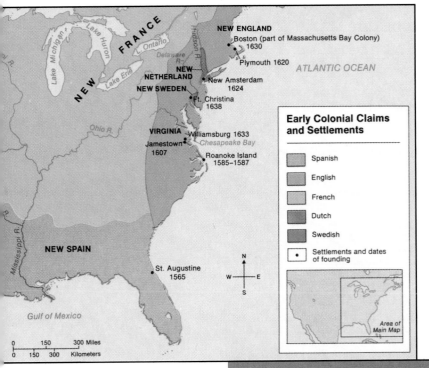

NEW ENGLAND
Boston (part of Massachusetts Bay Colony)
1630
Plymouth 1620   ATLANTIC OCEAN
NEW
NETHERLAND   New Amsterdam
1624
NEW SWEDEN
Ft. Christina
1638

NEW FRANCE
Ontario
Delaware R.
Hudson
Lake Michigan
Lake Huron
Lake Erie

Ohio R.

VIRGINIA   Williamsburg 1633
Jamestown   Chesapeake Bay
1607
Roanoke Island
1585–1587

Early Colonial Claims and Settlements

☐ Spanish
☐ English
☐ French
☐ Dutch
☐ Swedish
• Settlements and dates of founding

NEW SPAIN

St. Augustine
1565

Gulf of Mexico

Mississippi R.

N
W   E
S

Area of
Main Map

0   150   300 Miles
0   150   300   Kilometers

Think About It

Think about present times. What do people bring with them when they come to live in a new country?

Why did the settlers come to America?

Some Spanish people came to America to find gold. Other Spanish people came to teach the American Indians about the Christian religion. They were called **missionaries**.

Some French people came to America to trap animals and sell their fur. These people were **trappers**.

Some Dutch and Swedish people came to America to find land for farming.

Many English people came to America
to live and pray the way they wanted.

Some people did not want to come
to America. They were brought from
Africa as slaves. Many slaves worked
on large farms called **plantations**.

? Think About It

Why do people come
to America now?

The Journey to America

The journey to America was long and hard. Some people wrote about the trip in **journals**. A journal is a record of thoughts and feelings. Here is what a young person might have written about the trip.

June 25, 1680

Today is our 59th day on the ship. Last night there was a big storm. The waves were crashing onto the deck. I thought the ship was going to sink. I was crying. Other people were crying too.

The food here is old and bad. The water is bad too. Many people on the ship are sick. Some of them have died. Today, I saw some men throw a dead body into the water. That made me feel very scared.

I am sad because I miss my friends from home. I wonder what they are doing tonight. My parents say I will make new friends in America. I hope so.

Talk About It

Tell about your journey to America.

Beavers

Some people came to America as trappers. Many trappers hunted beavers. People wanted hats and coats made with beaver fur. By the late 1800s most of the beavers in America had been killed for their fur. Finally, laws were passed to protect beavers.

Beavers live in rivers and lakes. They have thick brown fur that looks black when it is wet. It is soft and shiny. Beavers have strong teeth and broad, flat tails.

Beavers use their teeth to gnaw through tree trunks. They can tear branches and bark with their teeth. They eat bark, twigs, and leaves.

Beavers use their tails in different ways. They move their tails to steer as they swim. They also slap the water with their tails to scare an enemy. Slapping the water surprises the enemy and warns other beavers to stay away.

Write About It

Work in a small group. Make a poster telling why it is important to protect beavers.

"When I Came to America"

Many children come to America
each year. Each child has a story
to tell about the journey.

This is Carlos's story. He was twelve
when he wrote his story. He came from
El Salvador.

When I was five years old, my mom came
to America. I lived with my grandmother. When I
was nine years old, my mom called. She said that
I could come to the United States. A man said he
would take care of me. My grandmother said that
I could go.

When we were near Guatemala, the man said, "Get out of the bus. We are going to walk from here to Xela, Guatemala." Everyone started to walk. We walked and walked for many hours.

Then we crossed a river. Some kids rowed boats so that we could get to the other side. We walked, rode a bus, and ran all the way through Guatemala, and Mexico, and into California. Finally, we got to Los Angeles.

Now my whole family lives in Virginia. We are happy to live safe in America.

 Try It Out

Show on a map or globe where you came from. Show and tell about the route you or your family took to come to America.

This is Sanel's story. He was eleven when he wrote his story. He came from Bosnia.

I came from Bosnia.
There is war in my country now. Many people are dying.
I am now in the USA, and it is nice here. I live with my family. There are seven people in my family.
I go to school here. I have friends. Thanks to this country!

Tell what you learned.

1. List reasons why the early settlers came to America.

2. Why do you think Sanel and Carlos are happy to live in America?

3. A time line shows when important events happened. Read the time line below about a student from India. Then draw a time line of your journey to America. Show when you left your native country and when you arrived in America. Include important experiences during the journey and in America.

We left India. We took an airplane.

We landed in New York. We visited Aunt Moulee. I saw my cousins.

Father, Mother, and I took the train to Springfield.

We moved into the Berkley Apartments.

I started 5th grade at Fairview School.

October 6   October 7   October 20   October 21   October 24

CHAPTER

8

Life in the Colonies

Tell what you know.

What did the colonists need to live here?

How did they get what they needed?

Word Bank

axe

hammer

nails

plow

seeds

wood

1

Talk About It

Which things are still important to build a home?

Jamestown is the first English colony.

In 1607, a group of around 100 men and boys came to America from England. They wanted to find gold and silver here. They started a town called Jamestown in what is now Virginia.

The people of Jamestown had many problems. They built their town near a swamp. The water was bad for drinking. Many insects lived around the swampy land. The insects gave the colonists diseases.

The colonists did not know how to hunt or farm. Many died from hunger and sickness.

The people of Jamestown asked John Smith to be their leader. He helped the people work together to survive. They began to grow food. They began to store food for the winter. A group of American Indians helped. They taught the colonists how to find food and plant corn.

John Smith

Talk About It

Did someone help you when you came to America? What did he or she do?

The Thirteen English Colonies

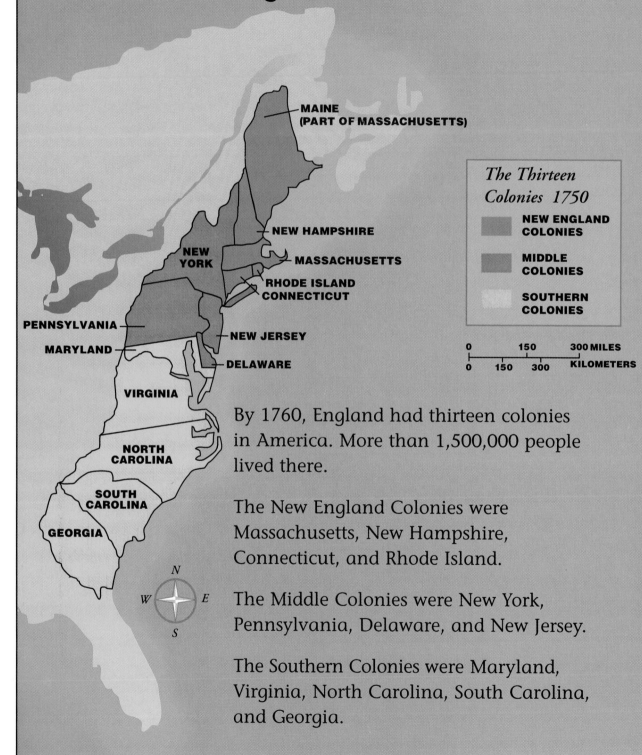

MAINE
(PART OF MASSACHUSETTS)

NEW HAMPSHIRE

NEW YORK

MASSACHUSETTS

RHODE ISLAND
CONNECTICUT

PENNSYLVANIA

MARYLAND

NEW JERSEY

DELAWARE

VIRGINIA

NORTH
CAROLINA

SOUTH
CAROLINA

GEORGIA

The Thirteen Colonies 1750

NEW ENGLAND COLONIES

MIDDLE COLONIES

SOUTHERN COLONIES

| 0 | | 150 | | 300 MILES |
| 0 | 150 | | 300 | KILOMETERS |

N W E S

By 1760, England had thirteen colonies in America. More than 1,500,000 people lived there.

The New England Colonies were Massachusetts, New Hampshire, Connecticut, and Rhode Island.

The Middle Colonies were New York, Pennsylvania, Delaware, and New Jersey.

The Southern Colonies were Maryland, Virginia, North Carolina, South Carolina, and Georgia.

The New England Colonies

Most of the people who settled in the
New England Colonies were from England.
They lived in villages like the villages
in England. They spoke English.

Many villages had a **meeting house**.
People used the meeting house as a church.
People also used the meeting house as
a town hall. They talked about village
problems there. They made new laws there.

Store

School

Meeting House

Common

Blacksmith Shop

Home

Talk About It

Is the place where
you live like the New
England village in the
picture? In what ways?

The Middle Colonies

The Middle Colonies had good land for farming. The major crop was wheat. Farmers sold the wheat in other colonies.

The people in the Middle Colonies came from many different countries in Europe. They had many different religions. They spoke many different languages.

The Southern Colonies

Storehouses

Main House

Stable

Farmers in the Southern Colonies grew cotton, rice, and tobacco. Tobacco was the most important crop. Farmers sold the tobacco to England.

The Southern Colonies had small farms and large plantations. Many people were needed to run a plantation. Some plantation owners used black slaves to do the work.

Think About It

Why do you think the thirteen colonies were all built along the coast?

Tobacco Sold During the Colonial Period

The Southern Colonies grew tobacco. They sold the tobacco to England.

Tobacco Exports to England During Colonial Period

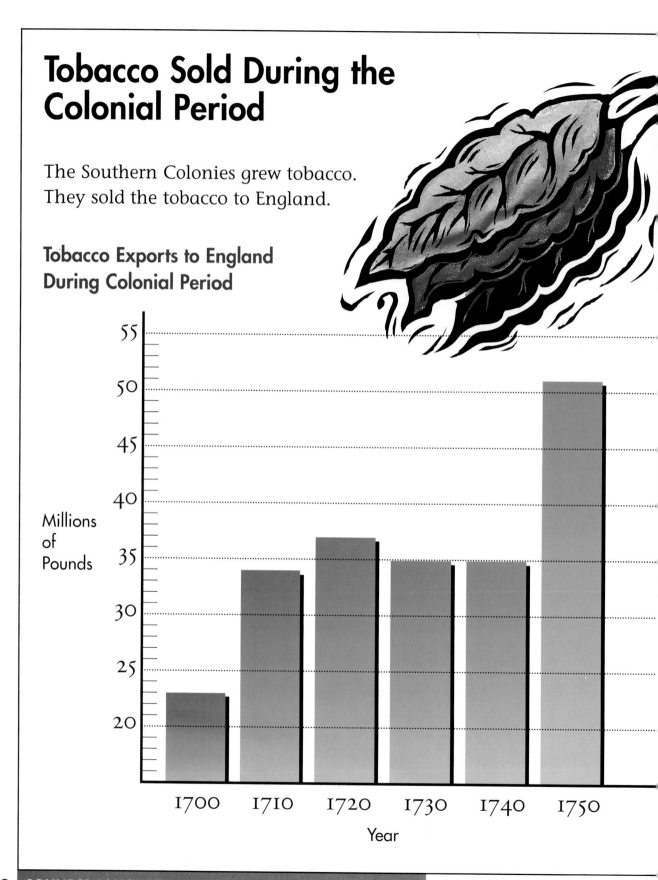

Millions of Pounds

Year

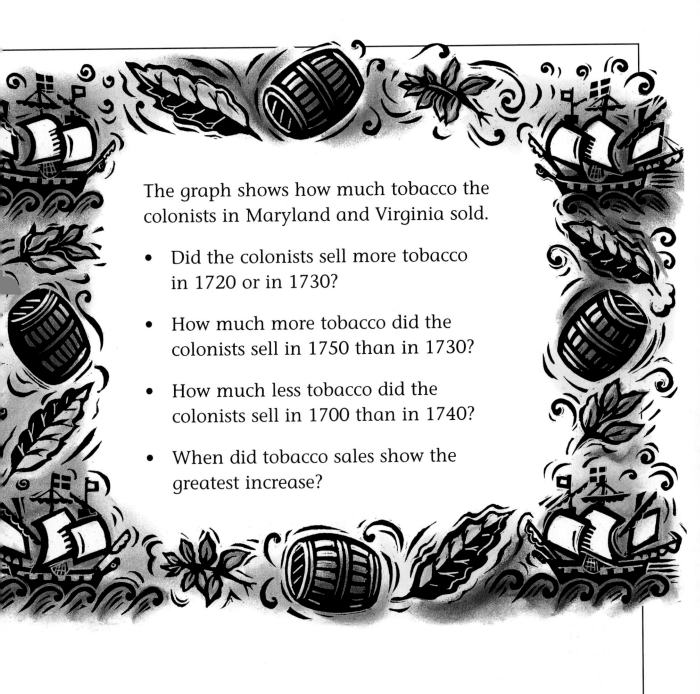

The graph shows how much tobacco the colonists in Maryland and Virginia sold.

- Did the colonists sell more tobacco in 1720 or in 1730?

- How much more tobacco did the colonists sell in 1750 than in 1730?

- How much less tobacco did the colonists sell in 1700 than in 1740?

- When did tobacco sales show the greatest increase?

Write About It

Work with a partner to write two questions that can be answered by the graph.

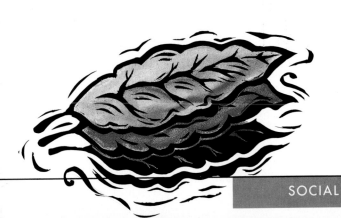

The Early Years of Benjamin Franklin

written and illustrated by Aliki

Reader's Tip
This story is from a book called *The Many Lives of Benjamin Franklin*. Benjamin Franklin was a famous colonist. He lived from 1706 to 1790. He was a great inventor and thinker.

Language Tip: Figure of Speech
A man with many lives means that Ben Franklin did many different things during his life.

Boston 1706

Benjamin Franklin was born with just one life. But as he grew, his curiosity, his sense of humor, and his brilliant mind, turned him into a man with many lives.

Benjamin Franklin was born in Boston in 1706. His mother and his father, who was a candlemaker, had many children. But they saw Ben was special. He was curious. He loved books. And even as a child, he was full of bright ideas.

Ben taught himself to read before anyone even noticed.

Ben's paddles were wooden, with a hole for his thumb. He made paddles for his feet, too.

Strategy Tip:
Use Pictures for Meaning
Can you find the paddles in the picture?

Ben was always thinking—even at play. He liked to swim, and tried different ways. Once he made paddles so he could go faster.

Ben loved school, but his parents did not have the money for him to continue. After only two years, he had to leave and choose a trade.

It was decided that Ben would learn to be a printer like his brother, James. So when he was twelve, Ben was sent to live with him.

Reader's Tip
When Ben Franklin was a boy, children did not have to go to school. Sometimes parents had to pay for school. Boys often learned special work instead.

Strategy Tip:
Use Context Clues
Ben learned a trade. He learned to be a printer. What does the word trade mean?

Strategy Tip:
Use Pictures for
Meaning
What jobs did
a printer do?

Ben's job as an apprentice was to clean and sort type, sweep the floor, and sell newspapers.

Ben spent nights and Sundays reading and practicing his writing.

Ben learned quickly. He worked long, hard hours. Still, he found time to read every book he could borrow, and saved the money he earned to buy more.

Later, he decided to go somewhere else, where he could write. So when he was 17, he left James and Boston.

Ben went to Philadelphia to start a life of his own. He found a job with a printer. He read and collected more books. He worked and saved until at last he bought his own shop. Now he could print his own newspaper and all the letters he wished.

Strategy Tip:
Stop and Think
What was important to Ben Franklin?

Ben worked very hard and even delivered his packages himself.

Language Tip:
Sequence Words
Later and *before long*
tell when things
happened.

A few years later, Ben met and married
a young girl named Deborah Read. Deborah worked
hard, too. She managed their new house, and her
own general store next to Ben's print shop.
Before long they had two children to help them.

Ben's father made soap and candles for Deborah to sell.

WILLIAM was the oldest.

FRANCIS was born in 1732. When he was four, he got very sick and died.

Baby SARAH was called "Sally" by her father.

Ben's newspaper was a great success.

Then he began printing a yearly calendar called Poor Richard's Almanack. The booklet was full of advice, news, and information. What made it even more special were the wise, witty sayings of Poor Richard. Year after year, people bought the almanac. It made Ben famous.

Strategy Tip:
Use Context Clues
To find out what an *almanac* is, read the next sentence.

Benjamin Franklin pretended Richard Saunders wrote the almanac.

"Poor Richard" was Richard Saunders, a poor astrologer who liked to spend his time gazing at the stars. His wife nagged him to get to work and make some money, so he decided to please her. That is why he wrote his almanac.

SUNRISE   SUNSET

Language Tip:
Figure of Speech
Living other lives means
Ben was doing a lot of
different things.

Language Tip:
Figure of Speech
Full of promise means
that a lot of good
things can happen.

Meanwhile, Benjamin Franklin was busy living other lives.

He loved Philadelphia. It was a new city full of promise, and Benjamin was there at the right time. He started a club called the Junto, where friends met to discuss books and ideas. He lent out his books, and soon others did the same. This began the first free lending library in America.

Men from many trades came to the Weekly Junto meetings.

Benjamin Franklin in his fireman's helmet.

A lamplighter walked through the streets at dusk lighting lamps.

He found new ways to light the streets, and to have them cleaned and paved, too. He started a police force, a fire department, a hospital, and an Academy. He helped make laws.

Philadelphia became as famous as Benjamin Franklin.

Language Tip:
Vocabulary
An *academy* is a school.

Language Tip:
Figure of Speech
A new life began means
that Ben started to do
something new in his life.

By the time he was forty-two, Benjamin Franklin had enough money from his printing to live in comfort with his family. He gave up the shop to spend all his time with his ideas.

A new life began.

Ben started scientific experiments, and soon became a master. He was the first to prove lightning was electricity.

One day, during a thunderstorm, he tried a dangerous experiment with a kite and a key, and found he was right. He realized how to protect houses from lightning, and invented the lightning rod.

People put "Franklin Rods" up on their rooftops in America and in other countries, too.

Benjamin Franklin's Dangerous Kite Experiment

He attached a pointed metal rod to the kite.

He tied a silk cord to the kite string and a key to the cord.

He and his son, William, took shelter. Lightning struck the rod.

He touched the wet key and felt a shock. Electricity had traveled down the kite string to the key. The silk cord stopped it from going further.

Language Tip:
Figure of Speech
Took shelter means "found a safe or dry place."

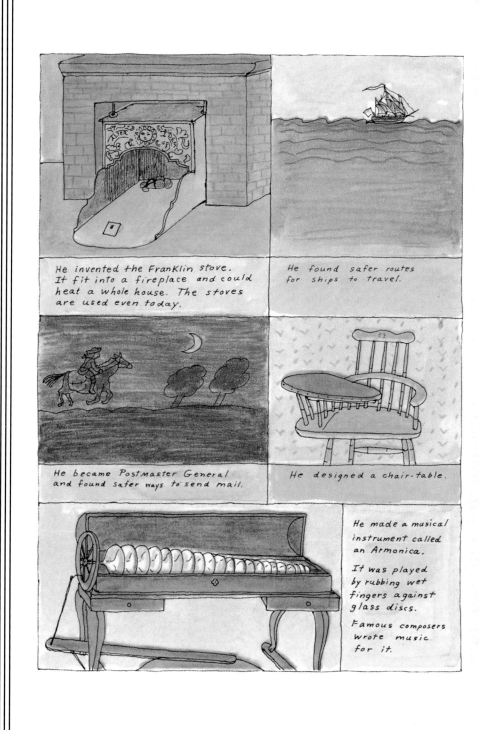

He invented the Franklin stove. It fit into a fireplace and could heat a whole house. The stoves are used even today.

He found safer routes for ships to travel.

He became Postmaster General and found safer ways to send mail.

He designed a chair-table.

He made a musical instrument called an Armonica.

It was played by rubbing wet fingers against glass discs.

Famous composers wrote music for it.

He experimented in his garden and found better ways to grow crops.

He invented glasses called bifocals. He could see far, out of the top of the glasses, and near, out of the bottom.

He introduced Swiss barley, Chinese rhubarb, Newton apples, willow for baskets, and turnips to America.

He found out that black cloth keeps one warmer than white by laying pieces of cloth in the snow. After some time, the black cloth was warmed by the sun and sank into the snow. The white didn't.

Benjamin Franklin made many discoveries in his lifetime, but he refused money for them. He said his ideas belonged to everyone. He wrote them down and they were translated into many languages. He became the best known man in America.

Strategy Tip:
Stop and Think
How did Ben Franklin's ideas make life better for people?

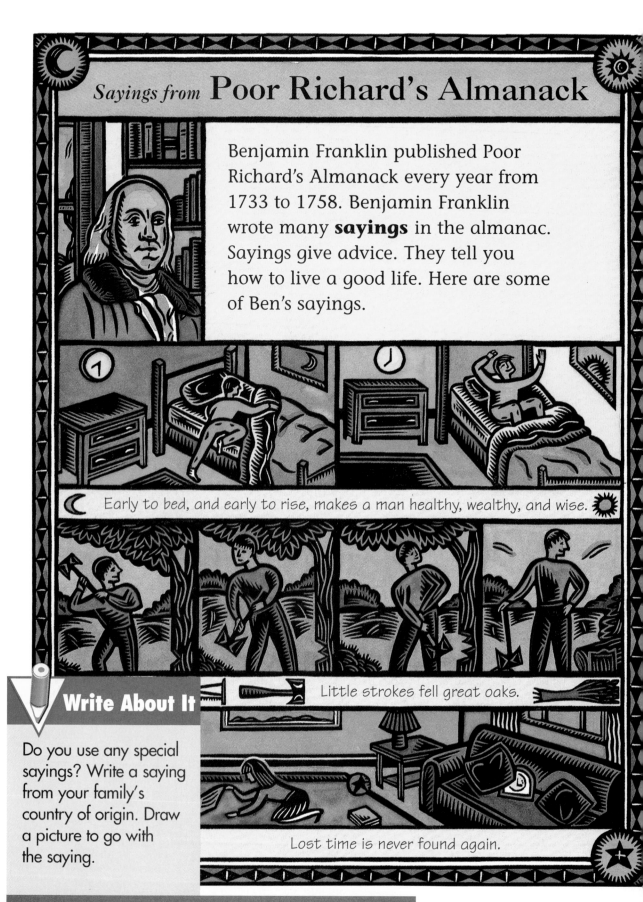

Sayings from Poor Richard's Almanack

Benjamin Franklin published Poor Richard's Almanack every year from 1733 to 1758. Benjamin Franklin wrote many **sayings** in the almanac. Sayings give advice. They tell you how to live a good life. Here are some of Ben's sayings.

Early to bed, and early to rise, makes a man healthy, wealthy, and wise.

Little strokes fell great oaks.

Lost time is never found again.

Write About It

Do you use any special sayings? Write a saying from your family's country of origin. Draw a picture to go with the saying.

Tell what you learned.

CHAPTER 8

1. People lived differently in the New England Colonies, Middle Colonies, and Southern Colonies. Which group of colonies would you choose to live in? Why?

2. What problems did the people of Jamestown have?

3. How did Ben Franklin's ideas change everyday life in America?

4. What did you learn about the thirteen English colonies? What would you like to find out?

What Do You Read?

Tell what you know.

What are these?

Why do people read each of these?

Word Bank

book

bus route

cereal box

letter

magazine

newspaper

sign

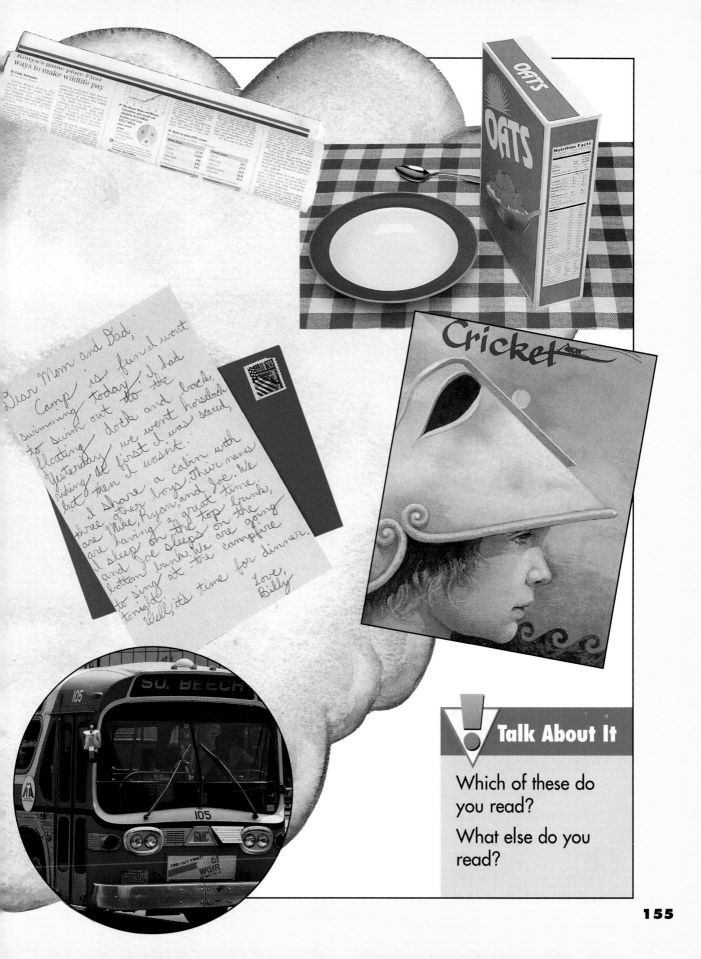

Kenya's game plan: Find
ways to make wildlife pay

OATS

Cricket

Dear Mom and Dad,
Camp is fun. I went
swimming today. I had
to swim out to the
floating dock and back.
Yesterday we went horseback
riding. At first I was scared,
but then I wasn't.
I share a cabin with
three other boys. Their names
are Mike, Ryan, and Joe. We
are having a great time.
I sleep on the top bunk,
and Joe sleeps on the
bottom bunk. We are going
to sing at the campfire
tonight.
Well, it's time for dinner.
Love,
Billy

SO. BEECH

Talk About It

Which of these do
you read?

What else do you
read?

Why do people read?

When you read, you can pretend to travel to other places. You can learn about ideas. You can learn about other people. You can learn about yourself too. People read for many reasons.

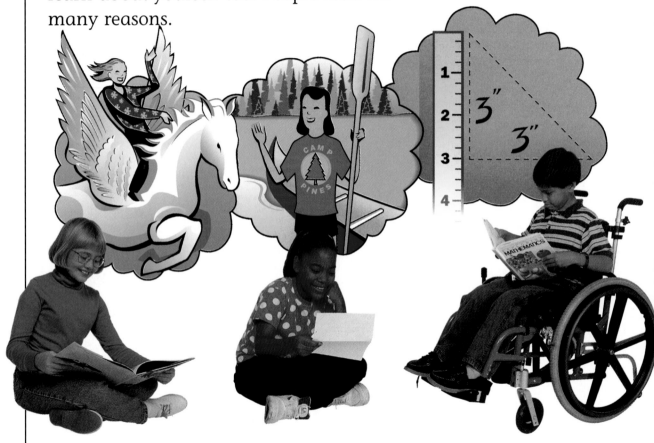

People read
to have fun.
They read books,
magazines,
and comics.

People read
to get news.
They read a letter
from a friend.
They find out
what the friend
has been doing.

People read
to learn.
They read books
to learn new
things and
to get new ideas.

People read to get information. They read newspapers to find out what is happening in the world. They read street signs to know where they are. They read store signs to know prices and what is on sale.

? Think About It

Think about what you read every day.

How does reading help you?

What are the parts of a newspaper?

The **front page** of a newspaper is filled with information. The most important stories of the day are on the front page. The name and date of the newspaper are on the front page too.

Look at the front page of this newspaper.

March 30

THE PARKER SCHOOL NEWS

Parker Elementary Is a Winner

Parker Elementary School won the city-wide reading contest. Parker's students read more than 2,000 books. The students won 50 new books for the school library. They also won a pizza party for all the students at the school.

Lynn Price, Juan Peña, Mike Berg, and Mai Lu are the top 5th grade readers.

From the Principal's Desk

See page 3.

♻ Printed on recycled paper

Number of books read	2,000		
	1,900	2,010	
	1,800		1,985
	1,700		
	1,600		
	1,500		
	1,400		
	1,300		1,565
	1,200		
	Parker School	Warren School	Lincoln School

article

headline

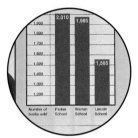

graph

photograph

Lynn Price, Juan Peña, M
are the top 5th grade rea

caption

Here are some ways the news is presented in the newspaper. These make the newspaper page interesting to look at and read.

An **article** is a story in a newspaper.

A **headline** tells what an article is about.

A **chart** or **graph** shows information in a visual way.

A **photograph** is a picture that shows something about the story.

A **caption** tells about the photograph.

Talk About It

Bring a newspaper to class. Show your classmates where to find the name of the newspaper, the date, a headline, an article, a chart or graph, a photograph, and a caption.

What are the sections of a newspaper?

A newspaper has many **sections**. Special kinds of information are in each section.

The **news section** has articles about what is happening in the world. News articles tell **what** happened, **when** it happened, **where** it happened, **why** it happened, and **who** was there.

WORLD TIMES NEWS

TOGETHER IN SPACE

ENTERTAINMENT

MOVIES
● 5:30 ● 9:30
● 7:10 ● 11:10

Kenya's ga
ways to ma

By Cindy Schreuder
TRIBUNE STAFF WRITER

MASAI MARA, Kenya—The Swahili word for enemy, "adui," long has been used as a synonym for elephants, lions, baboons and other animals that can kill people, destroy crops or make off with livestock.

Increasingly, however, these photogenic creatures might be better known by an American term: money-makers.

Kenya, with Africa's most restrictive wildlife protection poli-

growing realization that Kenya's parks and reserves cannot survive as temples of nature that admit only reverent foreigners.

"The parks can never stand in isolation, biologically. They will lose diversity," said David "Jonah" Western, director of the Kenya Wildlife Service, the government agency that oversees wildlife.

Protected tracts occupy just 7 percent of the country, insufficient to ensure the long-term survival of the large mammals and huge herds of wildlife for which Africa is renowned. Three-quar-

The **entertainment section** has information about fun things to do. People can find out when and where movies, concerts, and plays are taking place.

The **comics** tell stories with pictures
and words. They are fun to read.

The **sports section** has articles about
games such as football, baseball, basketball,
soccer, and hockey. The scores of the latest
games are in the sports section.

Talk About It

Which section do
you like to read most?
Why?

Which section is the
favorite of the class?

Story Problems

Word Bank

each

in all

less

more

take away

times

A story problem is a problem that is written in words. The problem can be solved using mathematics.

Reading helps you solve a story problem. Math helps you solve a story problem.

What are some math operations you can use to solve a math problem?

What are some clue words that let you know which math operation to do?

A school
has $270 to spend
on pizza for the students.

The pizzas cost $9 each.

How many pizzas
can the school
buy?

Here are some tips for solving story problems.

1. Read the story problem carefully. Say the problem in your own words.

2. Think, "What information will help me solve the problem?" In some story problems, you do not need all the information to solve the problem.

3. Look for words that let you know which math operation to do.

4. Then do the math operation to get the answer.

Write About It

Write a math story problem for a friend to solve.

Strange Creatures

by Alvin Schwartz

illustrated by Glen Rounds

Reader's Tip
"Strange Creatures" is from a book called *Kickle Snifters and Other Fearsome Critters* by Alvin Schwartz. The animals are not real. They are make-believe.

I t is said that there are strange creatures all around us—in the woods, in the mountains, in the lakes, everywhere.

Cowboys, woodsmen, hunters, and other people see these creatures again and again. Or say they do. Here is what they tell of them.

goofus bird

The goofus bird likes to see where it has been, not where it is going. So it flies backward. It also likes to sleep upside down. So it builds its nest bottom-side up.

rubberado

A rubberado cannot leap or fly, or jump or climb, or swim or swing, or walk or run, or creep or crawl at all. It bounces from place to place. And each time it lands, it laughs.

The rubberado also makes a tasty stew, but do not eat any. If you do, you will bounce and laugh and bounce and laugh and bounce and laugh for days and days.

Try It Out

Make up your own strange creature. Draw a picture of it. Give it a name. Tell one thing it can do.

Books to the Ceiling

by Arnold Lobel

Books to the ceiling, books to the sky.
My piles of books are a mile high.
How I love them!
How I need them!
I'll have a long beard by the time I read them.

Tell what you learned.

1. Think about all the things you read yesterday. Why did you read them? Make a chart.

What I Read	Why I Read It

2. Choose your favorite section of the newspaper. Draw or write something for that section. Share your work with a classmate.

3. Which strange creature from the story "Strange Creatures" on pages 164–165 was your favorite? Why?

What Makes a Good Story?

Tell what you know.

Do you know any of the stories on these pages?

What happens in the story?

The Old Ladies Who Liked Cats
By Carol Greene Pictures By Loretta Krupinski

THE GREAT BALL GAME
A MUSKOGEE STORY
RETOLD BY JOSEPH BRUCHAC
ILLUSTRATED BY SUSAN L. ROTH

Word Bank

exciting

foolish

funny

sad

surprising

wise

Talk About It

Tell a good story from your country of origin.
Why do you like that story?

Setting, Characters, and Plot

Word Bank

city

forest

island

mountains

seashore

town

village

Every good story has a **setting**, **characters**, and a **plot**.

The setting is where and when the story takes place. What is the setting of a story shown on pages 168–169?

The characters are the people or animals in the story. What characters do you remember from a story shown on pages 168–169?

The plot is what happens in the story.

Yayael and his parents in *How the Sea Began*

In lowered the gourd
(It spilled many beautiful
nourished. They had neve
silvery and still breathing
the cooked them and in
the meal.
The villagers rejoiced
"Salute Yayael" –We how
full stomachs,

▲ Yayael's parents
look in the gourd.

In *How the Sea Began*, the setting is the
village of Coabey. It is a place with woods
and mountains. The story takes place "in
the beginning of time."

The characters are Yayael, his parents,
four boys from the village, and the other
villagers.

Look at the above picture from the story.
What is happening? Your answer may tell
part of the plot.

Write About It

Draw a picture of
a setting in a favorite
story. Write about
the setting.

A Plot Diagram

What is the problem in *How the Sea Began*?

The plot is what happens in a story. The main character in a story usually has a **problem**. The character takes steps to solve the problem. These steps cause things to happen.

The important things that happen in the story are called plot **events**.

The problem is solved in some way. This is called the **solution**.

Look at the plot diagram on page 173. A plot diagram helps you remember what a story is about. It also helps you remember the characters and the setting.

TITLE: How the Sea Began

SETTING: Village of Coabey in the beginning of time

CHARACTERS: Yayael, Yayael's parents, four boys, villagers

PROBLEM: Yayael is killed. The villagers do not have enough to eat.

EVENT: His father puts Yayael's bow and arrows in a gourd.

▼

EVENT: The village hunters can't find enough food.

▼

EVENT: Yayael's gourd gives fish. Now the villagers have enough food.

▼

EVENT: The boys guard the gourd. They drop the gourd, and it breaks.

▼

EVENT: Water pours out to make a sea. The sea is full of fish.

▼

SOLUTION: Yayael's spirit lives in the sea.
The villagers will always find food in the sea.

Sometimes a group of characters has a problem. That is what happened in the village of Coabey.

Look at the plot diagram above. It is a diagram of the story *How the Sea Began* on pages 88–99 of your book.

Think About It

Would a plot diagram help you remember information in your science book? Why or why not?

Using a Plot Diagram with a Story

Look back at the story *Ben's Trumpet* on pages 26–37. Remember that the story is about a young boy named Ben who wants to play the trumpet. Write a plot diagram for the story.

In the evening, Ben sits on the fire escape and listens to the music from the Zig Zag Jazz Club. He imagines playing his trumpet. Sometimes he plays until very late and falls asleep in the hot night air.

▲ Ben plays his trumpet in *Ben's Trumpet.*

Answer the following questions to help you complete your plot diagram.

- Who is the main character?

- What problem does he have?

- What important things happen in the story?

- How is the problem solved?

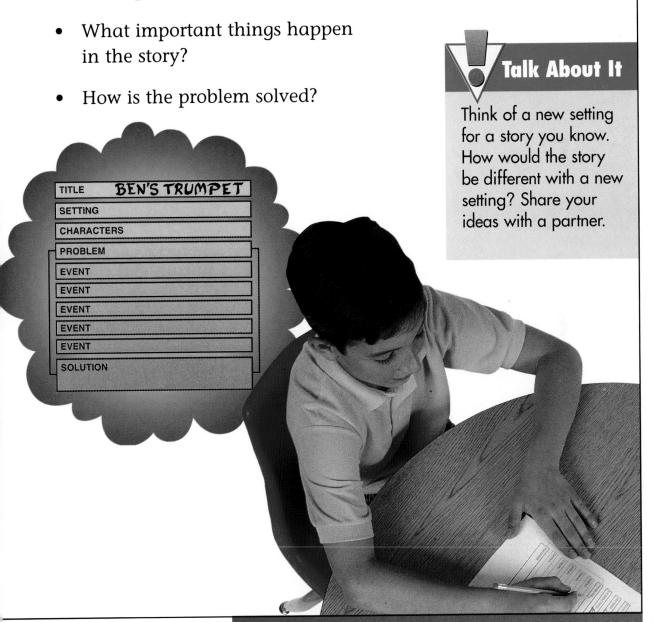

TITLE	BEN'S TRUMPET
SETTING	
CHARACTERS	
PROBLEM	
EVENT	
EVENT	
EVENT	
EVENT	
EVENT	
SOLUTION	

Talk About It

Think of a new setting for a story you know. How would the story be different with a new setting? Share your ideas with a partner.

Storytelling Around the World

People all over the world tell stories.
When people go from place to place,
they tell their stories to each other.
People in different parts of the world
have some stories that are alike.
Do you know this story?

Once upon a time
there was a young girl.
Her stepmother and
stepsisters didn't like her.
A magical helper gave
her beautiful clothes
to wear to a party.
At the party, she lost
her shoe. A prince found
the shoe. The young girl
married the prince.

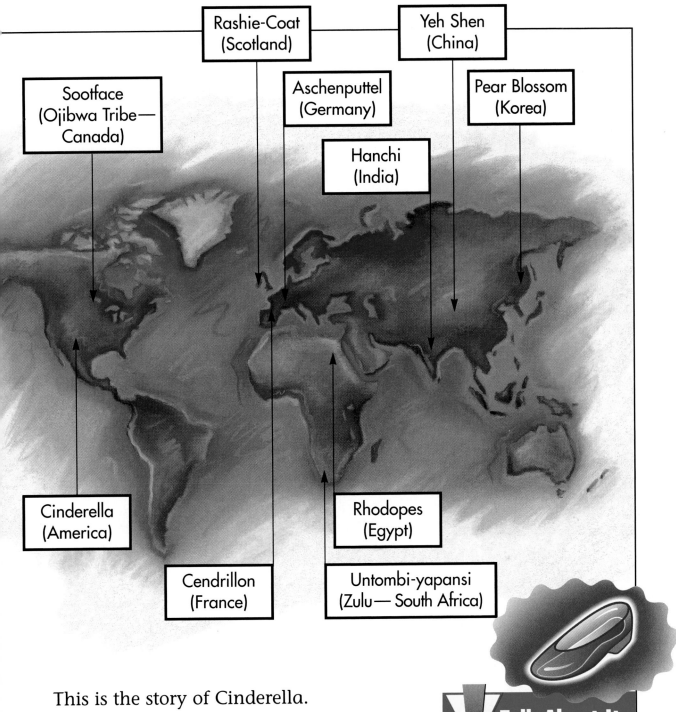

Rashie-Coat
(Scotland)

Yeh Shen
(China)

Sootface
(Ojibwa Tribe—
Canada)

Aschenputtel
(Germany)

Pear Blossom
(Korea)

Hanchi
(India)

Cinderella
(America)

Rhodopes
(Egypt)

Cendrillon
(France)

Untombi-yapansi
(Zulu— South Africa)

This is the story of Cinderella.
People all over the world tell this story.

Look at the map to see some of the
countries that have a Cinderella story.

Talk About It

Does your country of
origin have a Cinderella
story? Share it with
the class.

A Package for Mrs. Jewls

by Louis Sachar

Louis, the yard teacher, frowned.

The school yard was a mess. There were pencils and pieces of paper everywhere. How'd all this junk get here? he wondered. Well, I'm not going to pick it up!

It wasn't his job to pick up garbage. He was just supposed to pass out the balls during lunch and recess, and also make sure the kids didn't kill each other.

He sighed, then began cleaning it up. He loved all the children at Wayside School. He didn't want them playing on a dirty playground.

As he was picking up the pencils and pieces of paper, a large truck drove into the parking lot. It honked its horn twice, then twice more.

Louis ran to the truck. "Quiet!" he whispered. "Children are trying to learn in there!" He pointed at the school.

A short man with big, bushy hair stepped out of the truck. "I have a package for somebody named Mrs. Jewls," he said.

"I'll take it," said Louis.

"Are you Mrs. Jewls?" asked the man.

"No," said Louis.

"I have to give it to Mrs. Jewls," said the man.

Louis thought a moment. He didn't want the man disturbing the children. He knew how much they hated to be interrupted when they were working.

"I'm Mrs. Jewls," he said.

"But you just said you weren't Mrs. Jewls," said the man.

"I changed my mind," said Louis.

The man got the package out of the back of the truck and gave it to Louis. "Here you go, Mrs. Jewls," he said.

"Uhh!" Louis grunted. It was a very heavy package. The word FRAGILE was printed on every side. He had to be careful not to drop it.

The package was so big, Louis couldn't see where he was going. Fortunately, he knew the way to Mrs. Jewls's class by heart. It was straight up.

Wayside School was thirty stories high, with only one room on each story. Mrs. Jewls's class was at the very top. It was Louis's favorite class.

Language Tip:
Vocabulary
Fragile means "breaks easily."

Language Tip:
Idioms
By heart means "to know from memory."

Strategy Tip:
Stop and Think
Can dead rats live?

He pushed through the door to the school, then started up the stairs. There was no elevator.

There were stairs that led down to the basement, too, but nobody ever went down there. There were dead rats living in the basement.

The box was pressed against Louis's face, squashing his nose. Even so, when he reached the fifteenth floor, he could smell Miss Mush cooking in the cafeteria. It smelled like she was making mushrooms. Maybe on my way back I'll stop by Miss Mush's room and get some mushrooms, he thought. He didn't want to miss Miss Mush's mushrooms. They were her specialty.

He huffed and groaned and continued up the stairs. His arms and legs were very sore, but he didn't want to rest. This package might be important, he thought. I have to get it to Mrs. Jewls right away.

He stepped easily from the eighteenth story to the twentieth. There was no nineteenth story.

Miss Zarves taught the class on the nineteenth story. There was no Miss Zarves.

At last he struggled up the final step to the thirtieth story. He knocked on Mrs. Jewls's door with his head.

Strategy Tip:
Read on
Gravity is a science
word. Read on to learn
what it means.

Language Tip:
Vocabulary
A *spelling bee* is a
contest to see who
spells the best.

Mrs. Jewls was in the middle of teaching her class about gravity when she heard the knock. "Come in," she called.

"I can't open the door," Louis gasped. "My hands are full. I have a package for you."

Mrs. Jewls faced the class. "Who wants to open the door for Louis?" she asked.

All the children raised their hands. They loved to be interrupted when they were working.

"Oh dear, how shall I choose?" asked Mrs. Jewls. "I have to be fair about this. I know! We'll have a spelling bee. And the winner will get to open the door."

Louis knocked his head against the door again. "It's heavy," he complained. "And I'm very tired."

"Just a second," Mrs. Jewls called back. "Allison, the first word's for you. Heavy."

"Heavy," said Allison. "H-E-A-V-Y. Heavy."

"Very good. Jason, you're next. Tired."

"Tired," said Jason. "S-L-E-E-P-Y. Tired."

Louis felt the package slipping from his sweaty fingers. He shifted his weight to get a better grip. The corners of the box dug into the sides of his arms. He felt his hands go numb.

Actually, he *didn't* feel them go numb.

Strategy Tip:
Stop and Think
Did Jason spell the correct word?

Strategy Tip:
Stop and Think
Did Jenny spell the
correct word?

"Jenny, package."

"Package," said Jenny. "B-O-X. Package."

"Excellent!" said Mrs. Jewls.

Louis felt like he was going to faint.

At last John opened the door. "I won the spelling bee, Louis!" he said.

"Very good, John," muttered Louis.

"Aren't you going to shake my hand?" asked John.

Louis shifted the box to one arm, quickly shook John's hand, then grabbed the box again and staggered into the room.

"Where do you want it, Mrs. Jewls?" he asked.

"I don't know," said Mrs. Jewls. "What is it?"

"I don't know," said Louis. "I'll have to put it down someplace so you can open it."

"But how can I tell you where to put it until I know what it is?" asked Mrs. Jewls. "You might put it in the wrong place."

So Louis held the box as Mrs. Jewls stood on a chair next to him and tore open the top. His legs wobbled beneath him.

"It's a computer!" exclaimed Mrs. Jewls.

Everybody booed.

"What's the matter?" asked Louis. "I thought everyone loved computers."

"We don't want it, Louis," said Eric Bacon.

"Take it back, Jack," said Terrence.

"Get that piece of junk out of here," said Maurecia.

"Now, don't be that way," said Mrs. Jewls. "The computer will help us learn. It's a lot quicker than a pencil and paper."

"But the quicker we learn, the more work we have to do," complained Todd.

"You may set it over there on the counter, Louis," said Mrs. Jewls.

Louis set the computer on the counter next to Sharie's desk. Then he collapsed on the floor.

Language Tip:
Vocabulary
Collapsed means "fell down."

"Now watch closely," said Mrs. Jewls.

Everyone gathered around the new computer. It had a full-color monitor and two disk drives.

Mrs. Jewls pushed it out the window.

They all watched it fall and smash against the sidewalk.

"See?" said Mrs. Jewls. "That's gravity."

"Oh, now I get it!" said Joe.

"Thank you, Louis," said Mrs. Jewls. "I've been trying to teach them about gravity all morning. We had been using pencils and pieces of paper, but the computer was a lot quicker."

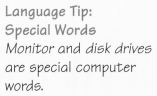

Language Tip:
Special Words
Monitor and disk drives are special computer words.

Language Tip:
Expressions
I get it means "I understand."

Reader's Tip:
Louis Sachar also wrote Sideways Stories from Wayside School, Sideways Arithmetic from Wayside School, and More Sideways Arithmetic from Wayside School.

Good Books, Good Times!

by Lee Bennett Hopkins

Good books.
Good times.
Good stories.
Good rhymes.
Good beginnings.
Good ends.
Good people.
Good friends.
Good fiction.
Good facts.
Good adventures.
Good acts.
Good stories.
Good rhymes.
Good books.
Good times.

Tell what you learned.

1. People in different parts of the world often tell stories that are alike. Why do you think this happens?

2. What are some of the unusual things that happened at Wayside School?

3. Make a plot diagram for "A Package for Mrs. Jewls." Use your plot diagram to retell the story to a friend.

4. What new information did you learn about reading in this unit? How will it help you read better?

Problems with England

Tell what you know.

This is King George III, the King of England in 1760.

What does a king do?

How do people act toward a king?

Word Bank

decides

governs

judges

leads

punishes

rules

obey

respect

!**Talk About It**

What would it be like to be a king or a queen?

Do you come from a country with a king or queen? How do you feel about him or her?

The colonies belong to England.

The colonists paid taxes when they bought molasses, cloth, coffee, and tea. They paid other taxes too.

In 1760, England had thirteen colonies in America. England's army protected the colonies. The colonists were expected to obey the laws England made for them.

Between 1764 and 1773, England passed many laws for the colonies. The laws made the colonists pay **taxes**. Taxes are moneys that people have to pay to their government.

England passed other laws. Only English ships could carry American products. Only factories in England could make some products, like wool clothes, to sell to other countries.

Many colonists became angry with England. They thought the laws and taxes were unfair. Some colonists wanted to decide what was best for America. The colonists had meetings to talk about what they should do.

Think About It

How do you take care of something that belongs to you?

A Tax on Tea

The King of England knew that the colonists were angry. He wanted them to calm down. He decided to take away all the taxes except one. He kept the tax on tea. Tea was a very popular drink in England and America.

This made the colonists even more angry. Many colonists felt that England kept this tax just to show them who was in charge.

The colonists did not want England's tea. In some cities, they did not let English ships into the harbors. Those ships sailed back to England with their tea.

The governor of Massachusetts said that the colonists had to obey the king. He sent a message to the angry colonists in Boston. He said that English ships would be allowed to come into the harbor. The English tea would be unloaded there.

Talk About It

Why won't the colonists obey the king?

The Boston Tea Party

It was 1773. The English ships came into Boston Harbor. During the night, one hundred fifty colonists dressed like Mohawk Indians. They put feathers in their hair. They painted their faces. They did not want the governor to know who they were.

The colonists got on three English ships in the harbor. They tore open the chests of tea. They threw the tea into the ocean.

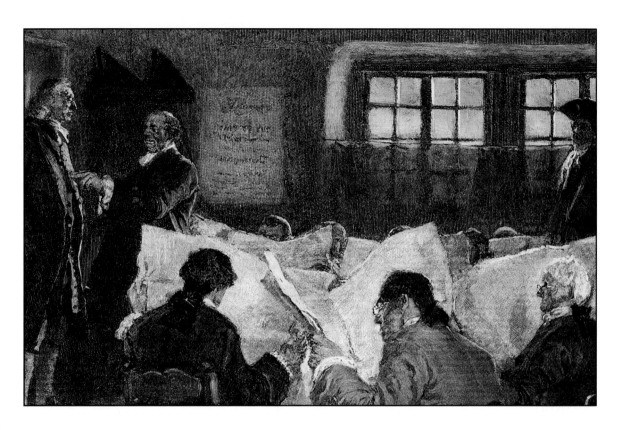

When King George heard what had happened, he punished the people of Boston. He said they must pay for the tea. He also closed Boston Harbor and sent more English soldiers to the Massachusetts colony.

But many colonists were proud. People in all the colonies heard about "The Boston Tea Party." The colonists knew now that they could do something. They could act together when England was unfair.

Write About It

Imagine you are a Boston colonist. Write a letter to King George. Tell him how you feel about what is happening in Boston.

Taxes

People pay a sales tax when they buy things. A sales tax is based on a percentage of the cost of what you buy. To figure out how much tax you have to pay, change the percentage of the tax to a decimal. Here's how to find 15% of $40.

First, change the percent to a decimal.

15% = .15

Then, multiply by the decimal the price of what you have purchased.

$40 x .15 = $6.00

You would pay $6 tax on something that cost $40 if the tax percentage was 15%.

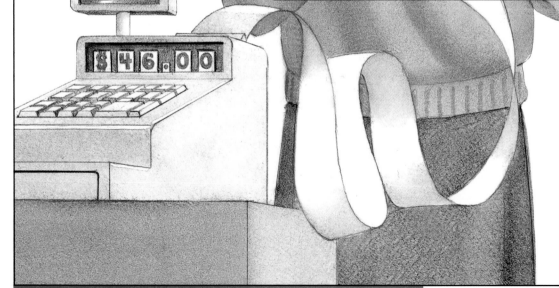

Here is a problem for you to solve.

Mrs. Díaz wants to buy a new jacket for her son. The price of the jacket is $35. The sales tax in the state where she lives is 6%. How much sales tax will she have to pay? Don't forget to change the percent to a decimal!

Sam the Minuteman

by Nathaniel Benchley

pictures by Arnold Lobel

Reader's Tip
Sam lives in Lexington, Massachusetts. The year is 1775. Ringing bells wake Sam. The whole town is awake. British soldiers are marching closer.

Language Tip: Vocabulary
The *village green* is the town center.

Reader's Tip
Minutemen were American farmers and shopkeepers who were also soldiers. They could get ready to fight in one minute. Sam's father is a Minuteman.

Sam got his gun and followed his father through the darkness to the village green.

The bells were still ringing, and a drum was making a rattling noise. Sam felt cold and afraid.

Captain Parker, the head of the Minutemen, told them to line up near the meeting house. Sam saw his friend John Allen. John looked the way Sam felt, which made Sam feel better.

"Why are the British coming?" Sam asked.

"They want the guns and powder hidden in Concord," said John. "They have to come past here to get them."

Slowly, it began to get light. The drums and the bells stopped.

"Maybe they won't come, after all," he said to John. "Maybe they'll go another way."

"Maybe," said John. "But not likely."

Then it was daylight, and the men began to relax.

Suddenly John said, "Listen!"

Reader's Tip
The Minutemen were hiding guns and powder for fighting the English.

Strategy Tip:
Use Context
Reread this page. What time of day is it? How do you know?

They listened, and in the distance
they could hear the sound of marching feet.
tramp tramp tramp
Tramp Tramp Tramp
TRAMP TRAMP TRAMP
TRAMP TRAMP TRAMP . . .
and THEN . . .

Over the hill and past the tavern came the soldiers! They came on and on and on. Sam could see their red coats and the sun glinting on their bayonets. They looked like a bright river of red.

As they came closer, Captain Parker tried to count them. There seemed to be a thousand. And he had only eighty Minutemen.

Language Tip:
Vocabulary
A *bayonet* is a long knife on the end of the soldiers' guns.

Strategy Tip:
Visualize
Picture the soldiers coming over the hill. There are many soldiers in red uniforms. They are marching close together. They all blur together into a big "river of red."

Language Tip:
Idiom
I'm all for that means
"I agree."

"There are too many of them," he said. "We had better move away."

"I'm all for that," said Sam. "I think I'll get on home."

"Me too," said John. "There's nothing I can do here."

Then Sam saw a British officer who was shouting and waving his sword.

"I wonder what he wants," Sam said.

"He told us to disperse," said John.

Then someone, somewhere, fired a gun—BANG! The troops began to shoot. Minutemen fell all around.

"Sam!" John cried. "I'm hit!"

John held his leg and fell down.

The British officer made his troops stop shooting. He marched them off toward Concord, leaving eight dead Minutemen.

Language Tip:
Vocabulary
Disperse means that the members of a group separate and leave the area.

Strategy Tip:
Stop and Think
What just happened?

Strategy Tip:
Use the Illustration
Check the illustration
to see that John was
helped home.

Sam and his father helped John's father
take him home. Sam felt he was having
a bad dream. He saw John's mother crying
as she put a bandage on his leg.

"How does it feel?" Sam asked.

"Not too good," said John.

When Sam and his father got to their house, all Sam's fear changed to anger.

"How did they dare do that?" he cried.

"Be quiet," his father said.

Then the bells began to ring again! The troops were coming back!

"Sam, you stay here!" said his mother.

But Sam had already grabbed his gun and run outside. His father followed close behind.

Strategy Tip:
Stop and Think
Why is Sam so angry now?

Language Tip:
Vocabulary
Dare here means "to do something bold or rude."

Reader's Tip
In colonial times, people rang bells to warn the people in the community of danger.

Reader's Tip
English soldiers fought in straight lines. The Minutemen could hide behind trees.

Language Tip:
Idiom
Their hearts weren't in it means "they didn't really want to do it."

By now more farmers had come from all around. They were shooting at the soldiers as they marched. They never got in close but fired from behind rocks and trees.

Then more British troops came out from Boston. For a while the battle was quite heavy. The British troops burned some houses, but their hearts weren't really in it.

Soon they headed back to Boston, followed on all sides by the farmers, whose bullets buzzed about like bees.

Strategy Tip:
Stop and Think
Did the battle seem
to be planned?

Late that night Sam and his father got back home. The rain was falling gently.

"Where have you been?" Sam's mother said. "I've been worried sick about you."

But Sam was too tired to answer. All he wanted to do now was sleep.

No one knew it then, but that day was the start of the American Revolution. The war lasted eight years.

At the end, America was a country on its own. But Sam didn't think of that. He thought of John and wondered how he was.

And then he slept.

Strategy Tip:
Step into the Story
How do you think Sam's family feels about what happened? How would you feel?

Language Tip:
Vocabulary
Revolution means "a complete change." People have a revolution to change the government.

Reader's Tip
The American Revolution is also called the War of Independence and the Revolutionary War.

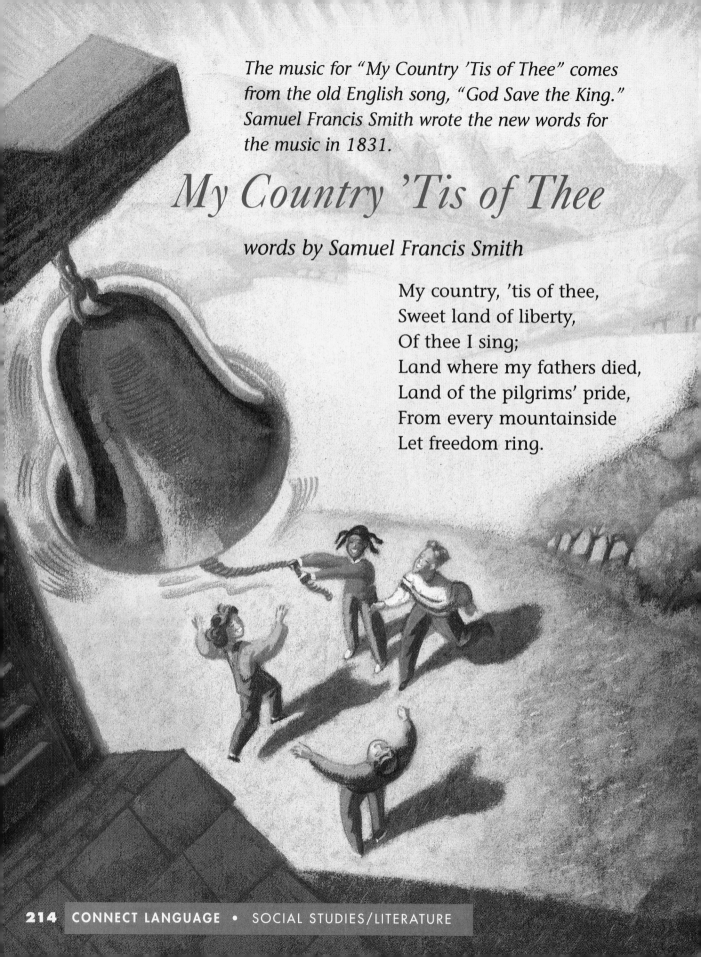

The music for "My Country 'Tis of Thee" comes from the old English song, "God Save the King." Samuel Francis Smith wrote the new words for the music in 1831.

My Country 'Tis of Thee

words by Samuel Francis Smith

My country, 'tis of thee,
Sweet land of liberty,
Of thee I sing;
Land where my fathers died,
Land of the pilgrims' pride,
From every mountainside
Let freedom ring.

Tell what you learned.

1. Why were some colonists angry with England?

2. Draw a picture of what happened at the Boston Tea Party. Tell a partner what happened there.

3. Think about *Sam the Minuteman*. Who would you say won the Battle of Lexington and Concord? Explain your answer.

4. What was the most interesting thing you learned in this chapter? Why was it interesting to you?

The War for Independence

Tell what you know.

These pictures show the American Revolution.

What do they show about this war?

Word Bank

boat

flag

general

river

soldiers

crossing

fighting

Talk About It

Do you come from a
country that has fought
for independence?
What happened?

The colonists declare their independence.

▲ Thomas Jefferson

Many American leaders were tired of England's laws and taxes. They wanted to have their own government.

Thomas Jefferson was a young colonist. He had good ideas about America. He had ideas about how it should be governed.

Thomas Jefferson ▶ stands as Benjamin Franklin reads a rough draft of the Declaration.

The American leaders asked Jefferson to write a public letter to the king. The letter would tell the king that the colonies were forming a new country. The colonies were no longer a part of England.

In the summer of 1776, Thomas Jefferson wrote the Declaration of Independence. Fifty-six American leaders signed it. Then they sent it to King George III. Soon, the new nation was at war with England.

▲ Thomas Jefferson presents the Declaration of Independence to the American leaders.

Think About It

How do you think the king felt when he read the Declaration of Independence?

What do you think he did about it?

General Washington and the Army

General George Washington was the leader of the American army. In 1777, the army lost two big battles. Washington led his soldiers to Valley Forge, Pennsylvania. The soldiers would rest there for the winter.

The winter of 1777 was cold and snowy, and the soldiers were tired and hungry. Many were sick. Their clothing had become rags. Some soldiers did not have shoes.

General Washington ordered his men to build huts. The huts would keep them warm. He asked the government to send food and clothing for the men. He taught his men better ways to fight as soldiers.

The winter was very hard. Many soldiers died. Some soldiers went home to their farms. But many soldiers stayed in camp. By spring they were ready to fight again. They were a better army.

Write About It

Work with a friend. Write a question that you would like to ask General Washington. You might ask about the war or about Valley Forge.

The Battle of Yorktown

The French government wanted the colonists to win the war. French soldiers came to America to help General Washington.

General Charles Cornwallis was an important leader of the English army. In 1781, his army was camped in Yorktown, Virginia. In October, the American and French armies fought the English army at Yorktown.

1773
Boston
Tea Party

1775
Battle of
Lexington and
Concord—
War Begins

1776
Declaration of
Independence

1777
Valley Forge

General Cornwallis did not have enough soldiers to win the battle. French ships would not let English ships come to Yorktown to help him.

General Cornwallis had to **surrender**. He told General Washington that his army would not fight anymore. Soon, the war was over. America was a free country.

1781

Battle of Yorktown

1783

Peace Treaty Signed

Try It Out

Make a time line of important events that happened in the 1700s in your family's country of origin. Ask your parents to help you with the dates and events. Share your time line with the class.

Using Capital Letters

Every letter has two forms—a capital letter and a small letter. Capital letters are "big" letters. For example, the G and the W in George Washington are capital letters.

The first letter in every sentence is a capital letter.

- *Tea was a very popular drink in England and America.*

The pronoun **I** is always a capital letter.

- *"I will help you," Sam said to John.*

The names of people and places begin with a capital letter. The days of the week and months of the year always begin with a capital letter too.

- *On July 4, 1776, the American leaders met in Philadelphia.*

Read the following sentence. Can you put capital letters where they are needed?

- *george washington's army slept in huts at valley forge, pennsylvania.*

Write About It

Write a sentence like the one above. Ask a friend to put capital letters where they are needed.

The Declaration of Independence

The Declaration of Independence states the beliefs of the first American leaders, the **founding fathers**. These beliefs are still important to the American people.

These are important words from the beginning of the Declaration.

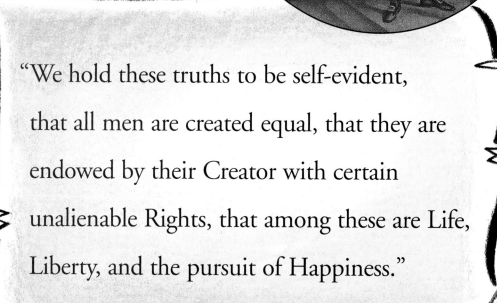

"We hold these truths to be self-evident, that all men are created equal, that they are endowed by their Creator with certain unalienable Rights, that among these are Life, Liberty, and the pursuit of Happiness."

The Declaration says that people have certain **rights**. Rights are based on beliefs about what is fair. The Declaration says:

- People have the right to live. The government cannot act unjustly to hurt them.

- People have the right to be free.

- People have the right to seek the things that will bring them happiness.

▲ You can see the Declaration of Independence at the National Archives in Washington, D.C.

Think About It

Imagine you live in a perfect country. What is it like there? What laws do the people follow?

YANKEE DOODLE

Yankee Doodle went to town,
  riding on a pony.
He stuck a feather in his cap
  and called it macaroni!
Yankee Doodle, keep it up,
Yankee Doodle dandy;
Mind the music and the step,
  and with the girls be handy!

A Yankee is an American. The English soldiers sang this song to make fun of the American soldiers. But the Americans liked the song. They sang it too. They were proud to be Yankees!

Tell what you learned.

1. Imagine you are a soldier at Valley Forge in the winter of 1777. Write a letter to your family. Tell them how you feel and what your life is like.

2. Why is the Declaration of Independence so important to American people?

3. Why did the English soldiers sing "Yankee Doodle"? Why did the American soldiers sing it?

4. What did you learn about the American Revolution? What would you like to find out?

① Prewriting

Choose a topic.
List your ideas.
Ask friends for ideas.
Look in books for ideas.

cities   jobs

coming to America   planets

computers   sounds

dinosaurs   sports

food   TV

Decide what you want to write.
Do you want to write a story?
Do you want to explain something?
Do you want to describe something?
Do you want to tell how you feel?

Writer's Workshop

Follow these steps to be a good writer.

Focus your topic.
Use a graphic organizer.
Focus on one idea.

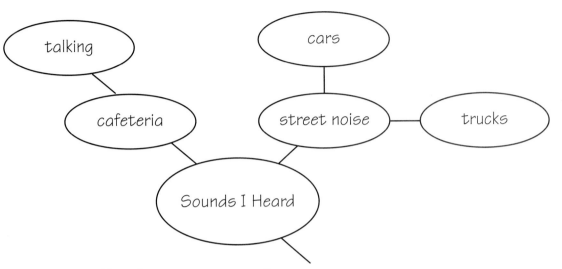

- talking
- cafeteria
- cars
- street noise
- trucks
- Sounds I Heard

Find details about your topic.
Look for information in books
and magazines.
Ask people for information.
Think about how things look,
sound, smell, feel, and taste.

② Drafting

Get what you need.
Get paper and pencils.
Get your graphic organizer.
Sit in a comfortable place.

Set a goal.
How much will
you write now?

Read your notes.
What do you want
to say first?

Keep writing.
Write down all
your ideas.
Don't worry about
spelling and
punctuation now.

Sounds I Heard

    Yesterday I hear many sounds. I see many
cars and truks on the streets Some cars were
honking ther horns. I saw a tall building too.
    At school, the peeple in the cafeteria were
very noisy they was talking. In muzic class,
everyone was singing. After school, I walked by
a park. the grant Park Orchestra was playing
muzic there I liked the drums and the trupets.
    I want play the the drums some day. I like
Loud sounds.

③ Revising

I think I need a better beginning.

Read what you wrote.
Ask yourself:
Does my story have a beginning, a middle, and an end?
Is my information correct?
What parts should I keep?
What parts should I leave out?

Talk with someone.
Show your writing to a friend or your teacher.
Do your readers understand your writing?

Why did you tell about a tall building?

④ Proofreading

Check your spelling.
Look in a dictionary or ask for help.

Look for capital letters.

Look for correct punctuation.

Make a new copy.

≡	**Make a capital.**
/	**Make a small letter.**
∧	**Add something.**
ℰ	**Take out something.**
⊙	**Add a period.**
¶	**Make a new paragraph.**

Sounds I Heard

    Yesterday I hear^d many sounds. I ~~see~~ saw many cars and truᵏks on the streets⌃ Some cars were honking ther⁰ horns.
   At school, the peᵒple in the cafeteria were very noisy⊙ they ~~was~~ talking. In muᶻic class, everyone was singing.¶ After school, I walked by a park. the grant Park Orchestra was playing muᶻic there⊙ I liked the drums and the truᵐpets.
    I want⌃to play the the⌃ drums some day. I like Łoud sounds.

⑤ Presenting

Share your writing.
Read it aloud to your family or classmates.
Make a book. Lend the book to your family
or classmates.

Sounds I Heard

Yesterday I heard many sounds. I saw many cars
and trucks on the streets. Some cars were honking
their horns.

At school, the people in the cafeteria were very
noisy. They were talking. In music class, everyone
was singing.

After school, I walked by a park. The Grant Park
Orchestra was playing music there. I liked the drums
and the trumpets.

I want to play the drums some day. I like
loud sounds.

What a Good Writer Can Do

- I can plan before I write.

- I can write about things I know. I can write about my family, my school, and myself.

- I can write stories with a beginning, a middle, and an end.

- I can ask others to read my work.

- I can write in complete sentences.

- I can put periods at the ends of sentences.

- I can make my handwriting easy to read.